THE GREEK PLAYWRIGHT

THE GREEK PLAYWRIGHT

WHAT THE FIRST DRAMATISTS HAVE TO SAY TO CONTEMPORARY PLAYWRIGHTS

CLEM MARTINI

PLAYWRIGHTS CANADA PRESS
TORONTO · CANADA

PLAYWRIGHTS CANADA PRESS
The Canadian Drama Publisher
215 Spadina Ave., Suite 230, Toronto, Ontario Canada M5T 2C7
phone 416.703.0013   fax 416.408.3402
orders@playwrightscanada.com • www.playwrightscanada.com

The publisher acknowledges the support of the Canadian taxpayers through the
Government of Canada Book Publishing Industry Development Program, the Canada
Council for the Arts, the Ontario Arts Council, and the Ontario Media Development
Corporation.

Cover and type design design by Blake Sproule

LIBRARY AND ARCHIVES CANADA CATALOGUING IN PUBLICATION

Martini, Clem, 1956-
The Greek playwright : what the first dramatists have to say to
contemporary playwrights / Clem Martini.

Includes bibliographical references.
ISBN 978-0-88754-875-8

1. Greek drama--History and criticism. 2. Dramatists, Greek.
3. Playwriting. 4. Drama--Technique. I. Title.

PA3071.M37 2009   882'.0109   C2009-904748-9

First edition: September 2009
Printed and bound by Gauvin Press, Gatineau

To Cher, Chandra & Miranda,
with appreciation and great love.

Don't worry about it. If God is willing, all will be willing.
After all, the God of General Salvation is
Right here on this spot. Here. He. You.
—from *Wealth* by Aristophanes

AUTHOR'S NOTE

Over the many years the oldest Greek playwrights have enjoyed and endured many different translations and adaptations of their works. These translations have varied greatly according to the attention paid, and the importance assigned, to diction, accuracy, idiom, metre, and rhyme.

As I have referenced the works of Aeschylus, Sophocles, Euripides, and Aristophanes in this book, I have employed a selection of translations, some traditional, some more experimental and modern. Some translators, feeling perhaps that the poetry and metre were critical, have attempted to capture these elements in their translation. Others, thinking that comprehension and ease of delivery were of greater importance, discarded rhythm or rhyme and utilized standard prose. I tend to believe that there is some benefit to be had from experiencing this diversity and have employed an assortment of styles.

This does present a challenge, however, because as varied an approach to text as the translators have taken, they have also applied to the spelling of names. Thus, Hecuba and Hekabe are the same characters, only in different translations, as are Clytemnestra and Klytaimnestra, and Pesthetareus, Pithetaerus, and Pisthetairos.

Where I have quoted from different translations I have elected to adopt the spelling of the characters used by the translators, certain that the reader would simply demonstrate flexibility, as the original Greek authors have, and adapt.

TABLE OF CONTENTS

BACKGROUND

PROCESS

LEGACY

FINAL THOUGHTS

PREFACE

If I was driving down a road and a directional sign along the way warned that the bridge ahead was broken—and it was written in Ancient Greek—I would plunge over the precipice. I'm afraid I'm a playwright, not a classics scholar or linguist.

My assumption is that most of the readers of this book will similarly not have read Aeschylus or Aristophanes in the original. If to appreciate these playwrights it's necessary to first master the antique tongue they communicated in, we may as well sweep their books from the shelves now and collect them in a very select archive, because the number of people with the ability to understand and read Ancient Greek amounts to a minute fraction of the living population.

I am a passionate lover of playwriting, however, and I believe one can experience something rich and profound through viewing or reading the works of Sophocles or Euripides without having first immersed one's self in the language of origin. And I also believe that the works that were written over two thousand years ago hold powerful lessons for playwrights today.

INTRODUCTION

The most distinctive feature of the Greek tragedy is also the most vexing for any modern company: the chorus. Every ancient tragedy has its chorus, and every modern production has to face the acute problem of what to do with a group of people onstage through even the most intimate exchanges of husband and wife, a group which has long odes in dense lyric poetry to deliver between the scenes of actors acting and events happening.... There is nothing more tedious and depressing in theater than a group of actors in white sheets intoning pompous banalities with profound expressions.

—Simon Goldhill,
How to Stage Greek Trajedy Today

The Suppliants, by Aeschylus, is a particularly boring tragedy whose only interesting factor lies in the culture one is able to glean from it.

—John Stinson, "Greek Theater,
Plays Serve as Sources of Greek Culture"

There is a prevailing sense in our contemporary culture that what the ancient Greeks did, thought, or wrote may be irrelevant.

Plays written by the ancient Greeks are felt to be wordy, nerdy, and dense; the outlook of their grim authors, humourless and bleak. The form they employed, with its lengthy monologues, vexing choral recitations, and references to arcane ancient practices is held to be impossibly remote. In a postmodern age when forms are readily shattered, scattered, spliced, and cloned, the Greeks are perceived to be too tightly bound to an archaic narrative structure. In short, the feeling is that the Greek classics are old, boring, and, in every way, yesterday's plays.

Part of this response may result from a failure of translation. Some early translators—overawed by the intricate construction, metre, and wordplay of the authors—rendered the text into a stiffly formalized, unnatural idiom. Consider the abstruse literary architecture and archaic, nearly incomprehensible phrasing of this still-employed translation of Euripides's *Hippolytus*.

> Great Zeus, why didst thou, to man's sorrow, put woman, evil counterfeit, to dwell where shines the sun? If thou wert minded that the human race should multiply, it was not from women they should have drawn their stock, but in thy temples they should have paid gold or iron or ponderous bronze and bought a family, each man proportioned to his offering, and so in independence dwelt, from women free. But now as soon as ever we would bring this plague into our home we bring its fortune to the ground. 'Tis clear from this how great a curse a woman is; the very father, that begot and nurtured her, to rid him of the mischief, gives her a dower and packs her off; while the husband, who takes the noxious weed into his home, fondly decks his sorry idol in fine raiment and tricks her out in robes, squandering by degrees, unhappy wight! his house's wealth.[1]

Part of our culture's response may equally result from preconceived notions of the classics, which have come to be most easily recognized in the myriad marble statues that stand erect in museums, are framed on the cover of textbooks, and embedded in websites. The expressions on the faces of these statues are terribly reserved. Their sense of barely repressed anxiety is reinforced by their stiff postures, still striving to maintain a fragile sense of dignity thousands of years after their demise.

For contemporary playwrights—very much concerned with sustaining a vital, energized art form—there is the worry that this inflexible, anxious mode of expression is no longer useful; that history will weigh too heavily upon the requirements of creativity; that the dead will, in a sense, overwhelm the living.

And, when all is said and done, it has to be admitted that the ancient Greeks are the very epitome of Dead White Guys against whom contemporary culture has rebelled.

All these objections contain a kernel of truth. They also ignore a couple of critical points.

---

1   Euripides, *Hippolytus*, trans. E.P. Coleridge, The Internet Classics Archive, http://classics.mit.edu/Euripides/hippolytus.html (accessed May 7, 2009).

Demosthenes, one of many Dead White Males on display. Photograph presented with the permission of the National Archaeological Museum of Athens.

The plays of the ancient Greeks still possess the capacity to inform and move a contemporary audience. It's not necessary to speculate on this matter—we know it's true. The works of Sophocles, Aeschylus, Euripides, and Aristophanes are produced on stages around the world every year. If you are a playwright that fact alone might make you sit up and take notice. A playwright knows better than anyone that getting a play remounted two years after its premiere can present a challenge, let alone two thousand.

As well, it's always a valuable exercise for artists to examine "firsts." By examining these initial moments of discovery one can sometimes detect the genuinely big ideas that lay the foundation for a discipline. And the ancient Greeks, as will be discussed later in this book, weren't short on firsts; politically, philosophically, or aesthetically.

Nor is it only the historical roots of the craft that are exposed by the study of the Greeks. Nothing ever stops exerting influence. The impact of Greek writers continues to be felt pulsing through contemporary practice today. To fully understand those influences, it's essential to return to the source.

More to the point, however, even if you are completely uninterested in the plays of the past, the *evolution* of theatre, from spectacle and ritual to a highly structured, complex dramatic form is of enormous importance. Not so much for how, but for *why*. Why did the Greeks, over a period of roughly two hundred and fifty years, develop a theatre that has for all intents and purposes become the template that Western societies have adopted ever since?

In this book, the emergent forces of early Greek culture will be examined for the precise influence they had upon theatre. In addition, the individuals most responsible for the creation of the craft of playwriting will be introduced and discussed, and their impact upon the nascent form calculated.

Sir Isaac Newton, in his letter to Robert Hooke, wrote, "If I have seen farther, it is by standing on the shoulders of giants." As individuals interested in the craft of playwriting, it makes great sense to me to have a notion of who the giants were upon whose shoulders we are standing.

BACKGROUND

1. THE CAST α'

Actually, it goes even farther than that. It's not just about knowing *who* they are, but having an idea of what made them gigantic in the first place.

There are individuals whose names surface again and again whenever the subject of Greek theatre is examined. It might be worth spending some time introducing them now. They are:

THESPIS
believed to have lived during the sixth century BCE

Greek history, at least as it applies to its playwrights, isn't a very distant cousin to Greek mythology. So little can be determined for certain from factual evidence, so much has been assembled upon a tissue of folklore, gossip, and conjecture, that it is difficult to parse the *absolutely* true from the only *probably* true.

It is, after all, only since the formation of written language, and along with that, methods of safely archiving and storing the resulting texts, that a dependable, verifiable history emerged. Greece certainly had developed the written word—at least a couple of times. Greek Linear B, the complex written language used during the Mycenaean period, featured over two hundred glyphs and signs. Perhaps because it was so complex, it was never widely employed and slipped into decline and disappeared sometime during the Greek Dark Ages. It was replaced by a form of writing that we know today as Ancient Greek, around 800 BCE—but there was no reliable, systemic method of archiving records. (We are told, for instance, that Aristotle's extensive lecture notes were essentially passed along from one person to another upon his death until they were eventually stored in a cellar in a small city in Asia Minor and then forgotten. It is on the basis of some very random acts and tremendous good fortune that we have access to any of Aristotle's writings today.)

The playwright/performer whose historical record most closely approximates myth would have to be Thespis. He appears to have lived at some point during the sixth century BCE. There are references of Thespis that come to us from Aristotle, but because Thespis lived prior to recorded history, much of what Aristotle describes as "known" about Thespis can only be understood as anecdotal and inferred. Aristotle maintains that Thespis was a singer in the dithyrambic rites (ecstatic songs or odes in honour of Dionysus, accompanied by dances and processions) but that he made adjustments to the practice of these sacred procedures and so became the first to actually act out the role of an individual character as opposed to performing anonymously as a member of the chorus. This individual role became known as the "hypocrite," or roughly translated, "the responder," and set the stage for something approaching what an audience today might recognize as dramatic dialogue. It is in acknowledgement of this that actors today are referred to as "thespians."

There are, in addition, a number of pleasant but rather unlikely tales related about Thespis: that he, in the spirit of invention, introduced masks to the theatre; that he introduced set pieces to performances; that he travelled about the countryside in a cart yoked to a donkey and presented a sort of peregrinating one-person performance. Plutarch, writing several hundred years after the fact in his *Life of Solon*, describes this lively exchange between Thespis and the renowned administrative reformer of the time, Solon:

> Thespis was now beginning to develop tragedies, and the attempt attracted most people because of its novelty, although it was not yet made a matter of competitive contest, Solon, who was naturally fond of hearing and learning anything new, and who in his old age more than ever before indulged himself in leisurely amusement, yes, and in wine and song, went to see Thespis act in his own play, as the custom of the ancient poets was. After the spectacle, he accosted Thespis, and asked him if he was not ashamed to tell such lies in the presence of so many people. Thespis answered that there was no harm in talking and acting that way in a play, whereupon Solon smote the ground sharply with his staff and said: "Soon, however, if we give play of this sort much praise and honour, before long we shall find it in our solemn contracts."[1]

---

1   Plutarch, *The Life of Solon*, in *Plutarch Lives, Vol. 1*, trans. Bernadotte Perrin (Cambridge, MA: Loeb Classical Library, 1914), 489.

AESCHYLUS
525/524–456/455 BCE

With Aeschylus, history moves to somewhat firmer ground. There is writing that can be firmly attributed to him, and a number of corresponding contemporary references to him. Apparently, Aeschylus was born not far from Athens, at Eleusis, the ancient site of the Eleusinian Mysteries—one of the older religious rituals in a country that has hosted many venerable religious rituals.

He was, as most male Athenians were at one point or another in their lives, a soldier and participated in some of the most renowned battles in Greek history. He is known to have fought—and lost a brother, Cynegeirus—at Marathon, a pivotal battle in the Persian Wars. It is speculated that he was active at Salamis and Plataea as well, although there is less concrete evidence of this.

It wasn't as a soldier, however, that he earned his greatest renown. His true vocation as a playwright was literally a "calling." That earliest of travel writers, Pausanias, observed this:

> Aeschylus said that, when he was a stripling, he fell asleep in a field while watching the grapes, and that Dionysus appeared to him and bade him write a tragedy; and as soon as it was day, for he wished to obey the god, he tried and found that he versified with the greatest of ease.[2]

Aeschylus followed the advice of his muse and enjoyed great success over the course of his lifetime.

The earliest example of an intact written play is his *Persians*. This play, based upon the famous naval defeat of the Persians by the Greeks at Salamis, was the winner of the first prize at the dramatic competitions at the City Dionysia Festival in Athens, in 472 BCE. It's as a result of the festival's clear records that scholars are able to determine a firm date for this important milestone.

As a consequence of his early participation in the development of the dramatic form, because of the literary strength of his canon, and because he is said to have taken the innovative step of creating the role

---

2   Pausanias, *Descriptions of Greece*, trans. J.G. Frazier (New York: Biblio and Tannen, 1965), 28.

for the second actor, as separate from the chorus (and so permitting actual dramatic scenes to take place between individual performers), Aeschylus is often referred to as the Father of Tragedy.

He enjoyed a long and successful life, and is rumoured to have died in Sicily when an eagle or vulture dropped a tortoise on his bare head. (Although this seems like another fanciful tale, it is not as unlikely as it first seems. There are, in fact, vultures that inhabit southern Italy that drop tortoises from a height onto the rocks below to shatter the shell and retrieve the meat hidden within.) He was survived by two sons, Euphorion and Euaeon, who went on to become playwrights themselves.

Aeschylus remained active to the end, however, and, depending upon the source you use, it's estimated that he wrote between seventy-three and ninety-two plays in his lifetime. This body of work compares very favourably with contemporary writers. To put this in perspective, Shakespeare, who was no slouch, only generated thirty-eight plays in his lifetime. The plays of the ancient Greeks were shorter, granted, nonetheless Aeschylus's work, by any standards, represents a serious corpus.

Unfortunately only seven of his plays have survived to today:

The Persians (472 BCE)
Seven Against Thebes (467 BCE)
The Suppliants (463 BCE)
Prometheus Bound (430 BCE)

And those three that constitute the trilogy, the *Oresteia* (458 BCE), for which he is best known:

Agamemnon
The Libation Bearers
The Eumenides

SOPHOCLES
496–406 BCE

There is more known about Sophocles than any of the other ancient Greek playwrights, largely because there existed a written document that was devoted entirely to his life. An anonymously written text titled the *Life of Sophocles* was found in the third century BCE. There is no certain way of ascertaining whether the biographical information was absolutely accurate or not, but most of the described events seem to conform to other surviving writings.

According to the *Life of Sophocles*, the playwright was born and raised at Colonus, a deme, or community, in Attica, and was a man of many talents. In fact, in some ways Sophocles can be said to have led a kind of charmed life. His father appears to have been an arms manufacturer and merchant who grew wealthy from the success of his thriving business. Sophocles lived during what is now described as the Golden Age of Athens. He knew and spent time with such celebrated figures as Pericles, Socrates, Aeschylus, and Euripides. Had he not achieved fame as a playwright, it seems likely that he would have found acclaim in some other discipline. His influential family provided him with the finest education of the time. As a youth he won prizes for wrestling and dancing. As an adolescent, he was chosen to lead the boys' choir in the celebration of the victory over the Persians at Salamis—a prestigious consideration. He was elected and served Athens twice as a general, was made Treasurer of the Imperial Fund, and later was appointed to a special commission to investigate the failure of the Athenian military adventure in Sicily. He was known to be pious. A temple devoted to Asclepius was installed at his home. In addition to all this, he performed at the festivals—but it is principally as a writer that his name has survived into modern times.

Sophocles's works became renowned in his time for their dramatic power and complexity. It was Sophocles's play *Oedipus Tyrannos* that Aristotle later described as best exemplifying tragedy, and it is this play, along with its match piece, *Antigone*, that have since gone on to become the most celebrated works of that time period. Sophocles's earliest writings have disappeared, the surviving plays appear to arise from his mid-career, but he is credited with having advanced the structure of tragedy by introducing a role for the third actor early in his career.

He too lived a long life, surviving both his mentor, Aeschylus, and his contemporary and rival, Euripides. He passed away at the venerable age of ninety. Like Aeschylus, Sophocles had offspring who grew up to become playwrights; his son Iophon and a grandson, also named Sophocles. It is a sign of the esteem that he was held in by Athenians that two of his plays were produced at the Lenea Festival shortly after his death.

It has been mentioned that the Greeks were prodigious writers, and Sophocles was no exception. It's said that he wrote one hundred and twenty plays, of which only seven remain:

Ajax (450–430 BCE)
Antigone (442 BCE)
Trachinian Women (450–430 BCE)
Oedipus the King (429–425 BCE)
Electra (420–410 BCE)
Philoctetes (409 BCE)
Oedipus at Colonus (401 BCE)

EURIPIDES
480–406 BCE

Don't you die for my sake, and I shan't die for yours.
—Pheres from *Alcestis* by Euripides

The mortal is mad who rests his happiness on the expectation of lasting welfare. Fortune is a whirling dervish...
—Hecuba from *Trojan Women* by Euripides

I have had for some years on my computer a file called "Unpleasantness of Euripides," in which I place at random, thoughts on this subject, in hopes that the file will someday add up to an answer to the question, Why is Euripides so unpleasant? Certainly he is. Certainly I am not the only person who thinks so.
—Anne Carson,
Grief Lessons: Four Plays by Euripides

If his world view was reflected in his writing, Euripides must have held a very low opinion of mankind. His tragedies featured suicide, infanticide, betrayal, orgiastic frenzied dismembering, and a variety of characters pushed to commit horrific acts by strong passions, by delusion, by fate, or by the arbitrary whims of the gods.

It's not surprising that this should be so, of course. The defining fact of Euripides's life was the Peloponnesian War, a bitter, debilitating engagement waged between Athens and Sparta that stretched over decades and ultimately sapped Athens of its prosperity and vitality. The surprising paradox is that at precisely the same time that Euripides offers up some of the very worst examples of human excess, he also displays a delicate, stripped-down eloquence, and characters who distinguish themselves by the manner in which they face horrors with courage and stoic dignity. The individuals that inhabit a Euripides play—and particularly the female characters—aren't necessarily nice or sympathetic, but they are strong-willed, passionate, and terribly independent.

He was a controversial writer in his time, and—as the above quotation from Anne Carson makes so evident—he remains so today. The last of the great tragedians of ancient times, Euripides was born on the island of Salamis. It's often reported that his birth coincided with the naval defeat of the Persians that happened off the shores of this island. As interesting as that coincidental happenstance would be if it were true, it's likely just a myth.

It would appear that his family was wealthy and influential, that he was exposed to some of the finest thinkers of the day, including Socrates and Protagoras, and that he loved words and writing. He was one of the first Athenians to be credited with owning a private library.

He was less socially inclined than either Aeschylus or Sophocles. It was said that he wrote in isolation in a cave—that can still be viewed on the island of Salamis—and that he crafted between ninety-one and ninety-five plays in his lifetime (this rough figure is arrived at as a result of the suspicion that some of the works may in fact have been written by the playwright Critias), of which eighteen have survived to modern times.

It would appear that he was invited to relocate to Macedonia by its king, and somewhere around 408 BCE he accepted this invitation. Some hint that it was a form of exile, some that he was discouraged by his losses at the theatre festivals—he received less acclaim and far fewer awards at the festivals than either Aeschylus or Sophocles. (After he passed on, and the Greek empire had been eclipsed, his work became more highly prized among citizens of the Roman Empire. There's a lesson in there somewhere about the ephemeral and arbitrary nature of popularity.) In any case, he emigrated/fled to Macedonia, where he wrote another two plays before—depending upon the account you believe—he was either devoured by dogs, or died from exposure to the harsh winters of the northern climes.

More plays of Euripides exist today than those of his writing peers because what appears to have been an alphabetically organized collection of his works was discovered. The surviving plays of Euripides are:

Alcestis (438 BCE)
Medea (431 BCE)
Heracleidae (430–428 BCE)
Hippolytus (428 BCE)
Andromache (425 BCE)
Hecuba (424 BCE)
The Suppliants (423 BCE)
Ion (418–414 BCE)
Electra (417–415 BCE)

Heracles (417–415 BCE)
The Trojan Women (415 BCE)
Iphigenia in Tauris (413 BCE)
Helen (412 BCE)
Phoenician Women (412–408 BCE)
Orestes (408 BCE)
The Bacchae (405 BCE)
Iphigenia at Aulis (405 BCE)

ARISTOPHANES
445–380 BCE

Well, here I am, and darn well ready to shout and heckle
and insult anyone who speaks of anything but peace.
     —Dicaeopolis from *The Acharnians* by Aristophanes

I entirely agree, said Aristophanes, that we should, by all
means, avoid hard drinking, for I was myself one of those
who were yesterday drowned in drink.
     —Aristophanes, as quoted in Plato's *Symposium*

Aristophanes can be seen as the prototype for the satirical writer—hard
living, hard drinking, opinionated, blisteringly caustic, and very, very
bright.

It's not exactly known when Aristophanes was born. His play *The
Banqueters* won second prize at the Dionysian Festival in 427 BCE
and he was assumed to be a young man then. The best estimate of
Aristophanes's lifetime has him born around 445 BCE and slipping from
the mortal coil around 380 BCE.

His works represent the only surviving examples of what is known
as Old Comedy. There are some who view his plays as an early kind of
frothy sexual satire—a Greek version of Georges Feydeau, the celebrated
French farceur. And I've read in at least one post-secondary study guide
that "Aristophanes wrote his plays to make the Athenian audience laugh
and relax during the wars with Sparta,"[3] which positions him as a sort
of Bronze Age "entertainer of the troops."

Both visions, I believe, seriously misrepresent his work. Of all the
playwrights, it can be argued that his was the manner that most closely
approached our contemporary sensibilities. His writing was nothing if
not edgy and provocative. He was lewd, yes, but he was also very political—and not in an esoteric or overly intellectual manner. His take on
politics was personal. He was confrontational and he held particular
individuals in positions of authority accountable. For him, nothing was
sacred. Some of his comedies—with their vulgarity, licentiousness, and

---

3   Sheffield Theatre Education Resource, http://www.sheffieldtheatres.co.uk/cre-
ativedevelopmentprogramme/productions/minotaur/theatre.shtml (accessed May 7,
2009).

profanity—could very comfortably be programmed at any Fringe festival today, or equally, could be produced as part of a political demonstration.

And he paid a price for his commentary. He was taken to court and prosecuted several times by authorities who felt his criticism crossed the line—at least once on the charge of defaming Athens in the presence of foreigners.

He was survived by three sons who also became comic poets, Aaros, Philippos, and Nicostratos. In his lifetime it is believed that he wrote forty plays, eleven of which are still with us today:

The Acharnians (425 BCE)
The Knights (424 BCE)
The Clouds (423 BCE)
The Wasps (422 BCE)
Peace (421 BCE)
The Birds (414 BCE)
Lysistrata (411 BCE)
The Women Celebrating the Thesmophoria (411 BCE)
The Frogs (405 BCE)
The Assemblywomen (392 BCE)
Wealth (388 BCE)

ARISTOTLE
384–322 BCE

Of the writers included in this book, Aristotle is the only one who is *not* a playwright. Nor, as far as anyone can tell, was he involved in the theatre in any special way. He was, however, a devoted teacher, a prodigious analyst and theoretician, and an individual with a hunger to determine exactly how things operated.

So why include his name among these others? Because he, perhaps more than any other individual from the ancient world, can be credited with creating an early *theory* of the theatre. That theory, based in large measure upon analysis of the works written by Aeschylus, Sophocles, and Euripides, literally altered Western culture.

After the Romans conquered Greece, the Romans transported their treasures back home and then promptly remodelled much of their empire upon Greek values. The Roman theatre can be viewed as having directly risen from the ashes of the conquered Greek theatre. And the critical writings of thinkers and analysts like Aristotle were assiduously copied by the Romans.

Following the decline and fall of the Roman Empire, the works of Aristotle slipped from sight in the Western world, but continued to be studied and discussed by Islamic scholars. When eventually Aristotle's notes, including those notes on the *Poetics*, were reintroduced to Europe in the Middle Ages, they had a profound influence upon culture and the arts of the time.

It would be an exaggeration to say that the work of Aristotle spurred the Renaissance, but his writings certainly influenced the architecture, the advancement of scientific and medical thinking, the religious practices, and the development of theatre of that time. The echoes of that first excited response can still be felt in the consideration and respect that his writings are afforded among artists and scholars within the film and theatre arts today.

Born in Stageira, Aristotle moved at a young age to Athens to study at Plato's Academy. After concluding his studies, he travelled, married, and was invited to the court of Philip of Macedon to tutor his son, the youthful Alexander (the Great). In 335 BCE he returned to Athens where he started his own school at the Lyceum. He established a particular style of teaching that became known as the "peripatetic school" from the Greek term meaning "given to walking about" because of his habit of strolling with his students as he taught.

He wrote widely, and apparently very well. What has survived represents only a portion of his complete works, and in fact it's not entirely clear if the notes we possess were actually written by him, or were simply dictated by him to a student scribe. In any case, it is now believed that most of what is archived today and credited to Aristotle was actually meant only as rough notes for his lectures.

He was an individual who had a seemingly inexhaustible number of interests, and he is celebrated in many, many disciplines for his thoughts on ethics, physics, philosophy, mathematics, logic, and biology. It's ironic that while the great majority of these writings were in fields outside the arts, and what he did write of the arts—the *Poetics*—is both small and incomplete, it yet holds a place of such prominence among the arts.

When Alexander the Great died, Aristotle left Athens. Aristotle may have felt that Athenians, resentful of the controlling influence of Macedonia and knowing that he was supported by and supportive of the previous regime, might possibly turn against him. He fled for Euboia, where he settled and escaped persecution. Ultimately, however, the trip proved too much for him and within a year he died.

Aristotle's work, as one can imagine coming from someone with such a wide variety of interests, is extensive. These are the essays and writings credited to him.

Logic
Categories
De Interpretatione
Prior Analytics
Posterior Analytics
Topics
Sophistical Refutations

Physics (the study of nature)
Physics
On the Heavens
On Generation and Corruption
Meteorology
On the Universe
On the Soul
The Parva Naturalia

Sense and Sensibilia
On Memory
On Sleep
On Dreams
On Divination in Sleep
On Length and Shortness of Life
On Youth, Old Age, Life and Death, and Respiration
On Breath
History of Animals
Parts of Animals
Movement of Animals
Progression of Animals
Generation of Animals
On Colours
On Things Heard
Physiognomics
On Plants
On Marvellous Things Heard
Mechanics
Problems
On Indivisible Lines
The Situations and Names of Winds
On Melissus, Xenophanes, and Gorgias

Metaphysics
Metaphysics

Ethics and politics
Nicomachean Ethics
Magna Moralia
Eudemian Ethics
On Virtues and Vices
Politics
Economics

Rhetoric and poetics
Rhetoric
Rhetoric to Alexander
Poetics

The Constitution of Athens

PHRYNICHUS — A CAUTIONARY NOTE

This is the reason why it is impossible to present a complete picture of the literature of this period, for only a tiny portion of the works have come down to us. Moreover, of all the works which were composed at the time, not one original copy remains.

—Suzanne Said & Monique Trédé,
A Short History of Greek Literature

Before one gets too cocky, or feels too certain about who should receive credit for what, one should take a moment to reflect upon Phrynichus.

A considerably lesser-known literary figure, Phrynichus was—or so it was rumoured—a playwright of some skill who antedated Aeschylus. In fact, he was considered by some to have been the *true* father of tragedy, and also a rival for the claim of having first created a role for the second actor.

According to the Suda, (an ancient prototype for today's encyclopedias) he was also the first playwright to introduce female characters—as performed by male actors, of course.

There is no writing authored by Phrynichus that has survived to modern times. None of his plays sit on the shelves of contemporary libraries. The world today is aware of him only as result of a few passing references made in ancient texts, but if he is viewed as a marginal figure in today's studies, and overshadowed by others, it is worth considering that this results from the slightest whims of fate, which dictated which scripts would be found, and which would not.

2. THE WAY IT WAS DONE β′

The past informs and shapes the present. To better grasp what the ancient Greeks have to say to playwrights today, it is worth considering how their works were intended to be performed in their day—which isn't as easy to accomplish as it first sounds.

If you're a historian of ancient Greece, the enormous benefit of studying plays is that at least you have actual, tangible, written evidence of the phenomenon. Understanding what the *productions* of these ancient plays looked like, however, is a whole other exercise.

There is remarkably little evidence to point us in this direction beyond the odd painted shard of pottery or oblique reference in one or another of the scripts.

This commentary from Allardyce Nicoll's *Masks, Mimes and Miracles: Studies in the Popular Theatre* offers up the kind of evidence that historians most often have to go on:

> ...the actors in the Old Comedy, itself an offshoot of Dionysiac merriment, adopted the padded costumes of the Peloponnesus. That they did so seems to prove definitely the existence of such costumes in early Dorian theatrical shows, and leads one to believe that the characters depicted on the Corinthian vases are not imaginative figures, but either pictures of actors in their roles or else inspired by performances of such actors.[1]

Some of the proofs depicted upon pottery appear to explicitly portray the theatre and are, in some cases, of plays that are still known and read today. One such krater, or vase, dated to 330 BCE portrays a columned building with what appears to be a platform or stage. Upon the stage stands an elderly man who holds a royal scepter. An older woman stands not far from him, and two young women. The older woman seems alarmed. This has been taken to be a representation of,

1   Allardyce Nicoll, *Masks, Mimes and Miracles: Studies in Popular Theatre* (London: Harrap, 1931), 45.

A ceramic mask mould possibly used by comedic actors. Photograph presented with the permission of the National Archeological Museum of Athens.

or perhaps inspired by, a performance of Sophocles's *Oedipus Tyrannus*. The older gentleman would appear to be Oedipus, the alarmed woman, Jocasta, and the two young women, daughters Ismene and Antigone.

Aristotle's *Poetics* offers some tantalizing glimpses of how plays were presented, making a number of specific references to productions, the way they were received by audiences, and where he felt they were most successful. His notes are mostly directed at the analysis of the text, however, and so naturally enough, they are relatively light on observations of performances.

There are other notes from which a vague portrait can be pieced together. Aristophanes, for instance, in his comedic monologues, often referred to one or another of the plays written by peers of his time. Some passing observations taken from commentaries, such as those of Plato, Herodotus, Thucydides, and similar contemporaries, have use. Nevertheless, the thread connecting pottery and the odd referential note to a complete vision of the theatrical world is, as you can imagine, very frayed—and there are a number of significant elements that, quite frankly, remain *unknown*.

The extent to which music played a role in the theatrical performances is largely speculative. It's known that the choruses sang, but there are some choral works that appear dialogic and some characters' dialogues appear to require singing. Euripides left behind what seems to be a kind of musical notation employing Greek lettering. As that notation is largely incomprehensible today to contemporary scholars, it doesn't shed much light on the issue.

Did women attend the theatre? There's evidence for either side of the argument. Some argue that there is virtually no record of a female *contribution* to the theatre. No female writers left scripts to posterity, no female critics left analytical opinions, and while there is some evidence of women playing musical instruments, and of women writing poetry, there are no references whatsoever to any female actors. At the same time, there are strong, complicated female characters that make appearances in the plays themselves. These female characters represented on stage are hardly retiring or passive. From Antigone to Lysistrata to Phaedra, they seem independent and completely engaged with activities of the time. And it's theoretically possible, although disputed, that women may have attended performances. In Aristophanes's *Women Celebrating the Thesmophoria* a female character, Mica, says this about Euripides:

> Ladies, by the Twin Goddesses, I've risen with no wish to promote myself. The reason is because I can no longer stand the way you've been besmirched by Euripides, the son of that cabbage seller, who's subjected you to a whole litany of slanders. What mud and mire has he not plunged us in? Where there's a theatre audience, tragic actors, and choruses, has he not slammed us with his vilifications...[2]

---

2   Aristophanes, *Women at Thesmophoria Festival* in *Aristophanes: The Complete Plays*, trans. Paul Roche (New York: New American Library, 2005), 498.

The implication is that women were present to *observe* these slanders. Theatre director Richard Sewell, has this to say on the subject:

> There is a canard that women were not allowed in the Theater of Dionysos, but they were; they contributed their presence. Women sat apart from men, as in many of our synagogues, where the separation is read less as a slight than as a signal of respect. Whimsical witness to Women in Aeschylus' audience can be inferred from the tale that the Furies in his Oresteia were so hideous that pregnant women miscarried at the sight. That anecdote would not have worked even as a joke if everyone knew that women were not admitted to the theater.[3]

Writer Peter Wilson finds the proof less convincing, however.

> We simply are unable to answer the "hard" factual question as to whether women were present in the audience. For decades scholars have squeezed the same few pieces of evidence for all they might offer, but the result has only been a lack of consensus; and a genuinely ambivalent picture emerges.[4]

So on this issue, the jury remains out.

It's clear that masks were utilized in the Greek theatre, but their origins and the way they were employed is anything but clear. Again Thespis—who becomes a bit of a catch-all as regards providing theatrical precedent—is sometimes attributed with introducing mask use. There is little evidence to support that, however. The masks were said to have been made of linen and wood, but because of the perishability of the materials, no actual mask has survived to modern times. What little is known of mask use again emerges from the paintings of theatrical representations on vases and the clay models on which it is assumed that masks were built, and the scant references to mask use that exist in the literature.

---

3   Richard C. Sewell, *In the Theatre of Dionysos: Democracy and Tragedy in Ancient Athens* (Jefferson, NC: McFarland & Company, 2007), 45.
4   Peter Wilson, "Powers of horror and laughter: The great age of drama," in *Literature in the Greek and Roman Worlds: A New Perspective*, ed. Oliver Taplin (Oxford: Oxford University Press, 2000), 109.

The following elements are fairly safe to assume, however. As of 534 BCE when Pisistratus, then tyrant of Athens, modified the Dionysian Festival, the dramatic component took on greater significance. It was at this point that the theatre competitions were established, which in a relatively short time generated a very loyal, very sizable following. At most major Greek sites of the Archaic period pursuant to the intervention of Pisistratus, you will find the temple, the stadium, and the theatre.

The actual, physical theatres were large, even by our contemporary measures, capable of—in some cases—seating thousands of spectators. They were built with the use of public funds, and this major expenditure seems to have been widely supported.

Throughout Greek history, as profane, challenging, and iconoclastic as the plays became, they remained an integral part of the religious ceremonies. It was not until much later that plays became considered a simple amusement to be produced for pleasure and entertainment.

Plays in Athens generally appeared at one of two Dionysian festivals: the Lenaean, celebrated around January, and the Great or City Dionysia around March. The Great Dionysia was the larger of the two, attracted a more cosmopolitan audience (dignitaries from foreign allied states

The Theatre of Dionysus at Athens.

would often attend), and was primarily programmed with tragic dramatic works. The Lenaean was smaller, played to a local audience, and apparently produced more comic works. Scripts presented for production at the festivals were first read and selected by an annually assembled committee of citizens, and were submitted in collections of four—three tragedies per playwright and an accompanying satyr play. (There aren't many examples of satyr plays to go on, the only extant script a play by Euripides titled *The Cyclops*, but it's assumed that these were a precursor to comedy.)

A choregoi (a highly respected, honorific position generally appointed to someone in the upper classes, somewhat equivalent to a theatre producer today) was teamed with each playwright. This individual was responsible for casting, organizing, and funding these sometimes very elaborate, very expensive productions. There was a good deal of excitement generated around the events, along with extensive preparations. Contemporary literature talks of choruses practising very hard for lengthy bouts of time. The festivals were competitive and, at the conclusion, the playwrights were awarded first, second, or third place. First place was, of course, very coveted.

The essential architecture of the theatre remained relatively uniform over the years. The audience sat out of doors in semicircular rows

A detail from the Theatre of Dionysus.

upon a raked incline. This theatron, or viewing area, was initially made up of wooden chairs or benches built and erected on a sloped hillside. Eventually this became formalized as the stone seating that can be observed at the more famous sites such as the amphitheatres at Delphi, Epidaurus, or the Theatre of Dionysus in Athens. The logeion, or stage area, where the actors performed, was slightly elevated above the orchestra—where the chorus was situated. The actors and chorus entered and exited through the parados, the alleyways on either side of the stage. Beyond the orchestra a scenic wall was constructed—the skene. It was behind this that actors changed costumes and, because it was considered inappropriate to show death on stage, it was likewise back behind this that the fictional deaths of so many tragic Greek characters were staged.

Various stage machines were employed by the end of the classical period, including the eccyclema, a kind of movable platform, and the mekhane, a crane devised to elevate and transport actors from the stage. This was the device most commonly employed in the entrance or exit of the gods. It grew to be so closely associated with a convenient or contrived ending to a play that it became connected to the Latin phrase still used today to describe an improbable device artificially resolving a plot: deus ex machina.

There's a tendency among contemporary society to feel smugly superior to the cultures of bygone days—we live longer, travel farther, have access to greater resources of knowledge, and generally believe that our modern way of life has progressed beyond that of cultures of the past—but it may surprise writers to know that however popular we become as writers we may never surpass the kind of universal popularity that the Greek playwrights enjoyed among their own citizens.

Plays among the ancient Greeks were exceptionally well attended. By the fourth century BCE, the City Dionysia accommodated audiences of fifteen to twenty thousand. Given that the adult male population of the time is estimated to have been somewhere in the realm of fifty or sixty thousand—the audience the plays most likely drew upon—the proportion attending the theatre can only be viewed as astonishing.

In any case, by the time the theatre was producing the major five-day spectacles of the City Dionysia and accommodating these kinds of crowds, it had been utterly transformed. From a minor supplement to a religious procession, theatre had been transformed into a complex mechanism principally designed to present and explore a new, visual, literate, textually rich style of narrative.

So, how did it get there?

3. SYNERGY,
OR, WHAT ELSE WAS THE WESTERN WORLD
DOING WHILE THEATRE WAS EVOLVING? γ′

Walk through a forest and eventually you'll come across a curious phenomenon. In the middle of a grove you'll spy a tree that differs markedly from the others. Instead of stretching vertically, it first prostrates itself to the earth, performing an elaborate, humbling curl before turning and once more extending upright.

It seems inexplicable that a tree should so arbitrarily twist and curl. The strange formation becomes understandable only if you then pass through an area where trees have been blown down in a strong wind. There you will find the odd toppled tree leaning against a smaller sapling, compelling the weaker tree to tip and tilt, and eventually to grow around and over the burden of the dead trunk.

It's then that things become clear. In the previous case, the older tree has since decomposed and disappeared from view. The younger has grown and, as it matured, retained its curious configuration as a kind of fossil legacy of the tree that once was, but is no more.

It's impossible to truly understand things in isolation.

To understand the way that the theatre evolved, it is important to reflect on some of the coinciding events that had influence upon it.

Even a passing glance at a timeline (see the appendix at the end of this book) offers an idea of the breadth of invention that occurred during early Greek civilization. Because society was evolving from simple, loosely connected agrarian settlements to more cosmopolitan, more sophisticated, more densely populated urban settlements, new ideas—by necessity—had to be tried and tested to coordinate and accommodate the sheer number of citizens living together in close proximity.

Naturally, each new invention and innovation had its influence upon the development of the theatre, some more than others. In this chapter those seven that had the greatest influence will be introduced, followed in the subsequent chapter by a more detailed discussion of the precise nature of the impact they had.

DEMOCRACY

To understand how the theatre flourished as it did, it's essential to be aware of the paralleling growth of democracy, as the two are so closely connected. The theatre often articulated the factional aspirations of its political cousin, the two shared common timelines, and from time to time they shared common bloodlines as well. Esteemed playwright Sophocles was also a highly respected Greek politician. Pericles, in addition to being the most celebrated statesman and first citizen of Athens's Golden Age, was also a choregoi at the Great Dionysia.

Greek democracy is generally acknowledged to have developed its first firm roots when Solon was elected Archon Eponymous, or Chief Magistrate, in 594 BCE.

Between the Mycenaean and Archaic ages Greek culture had undergone a radical change of administration, the causes of which are largely obscured by a period of time that is labelled simply, the Dark Ages. Where before kings had ruled—as Homer observed in his recollection of Agamemnon—the Greek culture contracted, became more focused around the polis, rid itself of its aristocracy, and explored new kinds of leadership.

By the mid-seventh century BCE, there had already been several unhappy transitional attempts to seize or concentrate power in the hands of ruthless individuals or small family groups. These efforts proved largely unsuccessful and polarizing. Solon was approached by the Athenians and entrusted with the authority to reform the economic and political systems and to resolve the social unrest. During his tenure as archon, he implemented a number of economic and political innovations. He forgave debts that had bound certain classes into conditions approaching slavery. He passed laws that permitted most citizens to be admitted to the ekklesia, a governing assembly of Athenians. From each of the four groups or tribes of Athens, a group of one hundred individuals were selected to form the boule, or council of four hundred, which provided direction to the ekklesia. By permitting most people (not all—neither slaves nor women were afforded a say), including the lower economic classes, a stake in governance, he laid a lasting foundation for democracy.

This movement toward a collective sharing of power was further advanced by the renowned political reformer Cleisthenes in 509 BCE, who first helped to dispose of the tyranny that had re-entrenched itself following Solon and then, in his role as archon, reorganized Athens along more democratic principles. He first restructured the tribes of Athens along geographic rather that tribal lines, and opened it up to a larger pool of participants. He subsequently created a legislative body that selected members through a lottery system and so more fully engaged a broader spectrum of Athenian society in governance.

These efforts to create a more open and inclusive democratic system proved popular among Athenians of the time, but highly controversial in outlying regions. Many less permissive societies were located in close proximity to the Attican community. (Sparta, for instance, a scant few hundreds of miles away, operated upon a much more extensive, systemic use of slavery, and was governed by a powerful military class and a hereditary ruling aristocracy.) For cultures that relied upon the continued labours of a fiercely repressed population, the very existence, and temptation, of a more open and liberal society was considered threatening.

This socio-political experiment provoked intense debate and tension among societies throughout those nations bordering the Mediterranean. Ultimately the same concerns and anxieties that propelled the evolving democratic revolution forward would also serve to advance the formation of theatre.

It is perhaps no surprise that this should be so. The apprehensions and aspirations of a strong and vibrant culture should be expected to materialize in the emerging literature/art of the times, and that certainly proved to be the case in the Greek dramatic form. In Aeschylus's *The Persians*, for instance, one can detect a stern condemnation of the Persian military dictatorship and a celebration of the triumph of the rather less organized, democratic Greek underdog. In Sophocles's *Antigone* the protagonist demonstrates her disdain for the rigidity and essentially anti-human spirit of dictatorship, and in *The Acharnians* by Aristophanes, or his later work *Lysistrata*, there are explicit expressions of support for democracy.

I will argue, however, that the influence of this democratic sentiment went far beyond simply generating content for the plays of the time, but in fact extended to shaping the structure, nature, and integral operating mechanisms of the dramatic form.

THE OLYMPICS

Because of its ancient pedigree, the precise age of the Olympic Games is almost impossible to determine with any degree of certainty. In the *Odyssey*, now assumed to have been written sometime in the eighth or possibly ninth century BCE, the writer (or writers, depending upon whether you conform to the single Homeric source or multiple source theories), Homer, mentions athletic games that sound very much like those events staged later at the Olympics.

Pausanias writes that:

> With regard to the Olympic games, the Elean antiquaries say that Cronus first reigned in heaven, and that a temple was made for him at Olympia by the men of that age, who were named the Golden race; and that when Zeus was born, Rhea committed the safekeeping of the child to the Idaean Dactyls of Curetes... some say that Zeus here wrestled with Cronus himself for the kingdom; others that he held the games in honour of his victory over Cronus. Amongst those who are said to have victories is Apollo, who is related to have outrun Hermes in a race, and to have vanquished Ares in boxing.[1]

The first definitively recorded games were hosted in Olympia in 776 BCE. The sole event featured at this first festival: the foot race. The concept of honour was an integral part of the early Olympic Games. Officially, the winner of any event received only a garland of olives branches as a reward for his efforts. (Although in reality the position of privilege that the winner received was considerable, accompanied as the award was, by a number of very attractive financial incentives.) Over the next four hundred years the games continued to evolve, develop, and expand, adding events to the menu, including the long-distance race in 720 BCE, boxing in 688 BCE, and the race in armour in 520 BCE.

Although these matters will be taken up in greater detail in the subsequent chapter, it is interesting to consider how similar the theatre and sporting events now appear. Both were performative in that a select group of participants staged something for the benefit of an audience. Both were temporal events in that they were firmly defined by a

---

1   Pausanias, *Descriptions of Greece*, 245.

highly structured beginning, middle, and end. In each case the audiences attended the events to observe certain struggles, struggles which grew more intense over the course of the performance, and the outcomes of which were defining moments for the participants.

The site of the Ancient Olympics at Olympia.

LITERACY

Although it may seem an oversimplification to state that the invention and dissemination of a written alphabet gave rise to the theatre, the development of the written word certainly had a profound influence upon all of ancient Greek culture, including the theatre.

The nature of writing about a thing changes the nature of that thing—and this is particularly true of storytelling. As stories that had previously only been delivered orally were recorded as written text, not only did the stories stop evolving and adapting in their performances, but following the decline of the oral tradition and the ascendancy of writing, stories were approached with a fixed, immutable, resolutely *written* end in sight from the very beginning.

Jennifer Wise argues persuasively in *The Invention of Theatre* that the abilities generated by reading and writing created unique conditions that made theatre possible. She offers two particular arenas that literacy opened up to playwrights.

The first had to do with invention. Because the written word did not require the services of a "teller," but instead could be enjoyed anonymously—and severally—by any number of readers, it meant that stories could be shared, compiled, stored, or distributed and consequently a greater number of stories were desired. And because the stories were recorded on paper it meant that the writer would not be required to demonstrate virtuosic skills of memory, or carefully and habitually attend to the practice and performance of a time-limited number of traditional sagas; and consequently writers were at liberty to generate *new* stories and *new approaches* to old stories. In fact, Wise suggests that the process of generating new material overtook the performance of traditional material:

> As a particularly powerful symbol of this new literate concern with narrative novelty, competition in drama, unlike rhapsodic contest, demanded the creation of large quantities of brand new poems, year after year. The oral poet must conserve, the literate poet, as Aristotle nagged, must show invention, he must offer his audience something new.[2]

---

2   Jennifer Wise, *Dionysus Writes: The Invention of Theatre in Ancient Greece* (Ithaca, NY: Cornell University Press, 1998), 60.

The impact of an alphabetized mode of writing on a bardic tradition was quickly apparent. Prior to the development of the written word, the works of Homer were offered as a kind of paradigm. Homeric works were repeatedly performed by storytellers at a host of festivals scattered throughout the Mediterranean. Once the tools of the written language appeared, however, so too followed an avalanche of newly generated stories.

Along with the ability to generate a new story, another skill set was introduced as a result of the advancement of the written word—this time the skill to more accurately capture and represent the spoken word as a specific, character-generated series of dialogues:

> Because the representation of speech in epic is controlled by metrical and formulaic consistency demanded by an oral mode, a fictional character in the hands of an oral storyteller can be represented as saying only what the available metrical units in a line will permit, and all speeches are largely determined in advance by the existence of a tried-and-true scheme. For this reason, speech as represented by the oral means of the epic is not particularized beyond the point of basic pragmatics: uttering of a threat, the offering of thanks, the announcement of a wish to die at once.
>
> Furthermore, the homogeneity of speech as represented in epic is but a kind of symptom of the fact that the bard speaks in his own voice for all characters.[3]

Even a brief survey of Homer's *Iliad* and *Odyssey* makes it obvious that characters in this form are much more clearly defined by the actions that they take than by the dialogue they employ. Odysseus is better remembered for the courageous decisions he makes on behalf of his crew as he guides them across the sea, or the cunning actions he initiates to drive out the suitors and win back his home, than for anything he says— or for *how* he says it. In fact, the lines of dialogue, such as they are, are relatively general and as regards character, almost interchangeable.

These opportunities, emerging as a result of the development of writing, provided a fresh methodology for approaching story. The new approach would have implications upon the kinds of tales that might be portrayed in the theatre, and the ways that characters could be represented in those tales.

---

3   Ibid., 29–30.

RHETORIC

From as early as Homer... the Greeks placed a high value on effective speaking. Even Achilles, whose greatness was primarily established on the battlefield, was brought up to be "a speaker of words and a doer of deeds" (*Iliad* 9:443); and Athenian leaders of the sixth and fifth centuries, such as Solon, Themistocles, and Pericles, were all accomplished orators. Most Greek literary genres—notably epic tragedy and history—underscore the importance of oratory by their inclusion of set speeches.
—Michael Gagarin, "Greek Oratory"

This is an age when the world is subjected to a set of rules. The fifth century in particular sees the rise of the techne, the technical manual. Within this intellectual trend it is not surprising that oratory too was gradually systematized.
—Chris Carey,
"Observers of Speeches and Hearers of Action"

The Greeks, from earliest times, regarded the ability to utilize language to explain, excite, and persuade as a skill of importance. Following the political reforms instituted by Solon, the talents of persuasion took on greater weight.

After all, the ability to speak clearly and argue persuasively would prove to be one of the essential skills in a young democracy. If people were to be kept apprised of events sufficiently to make informed decisions, it would be through clear speech. If difficult measures were to be taken based upon the decisions made by the many, then it would be essential that individuals be able to argue their cases and persuade their peers.

A number of lecturers of that time became famous for their instruction regarding rhetorical skills, including Protagoras, Gorgias, and Isocrates. Aristotle felt it was sufficiently important a topic that he devoted a major section of his writing to the *Art of Rhetoric*. It's significant that as the Greeks developed the art of persuasion, they also felt that the true character of the speaker might be more fully exposed through the use of rhetoric. In fact, it was felt that transparency of character might be useful for a speaker inasmuch as an honest or good person could reasonably be trusted by an audience more than a deceitful individual.

The trouble was that rhetoric didn't necessarily operate that way. There were times when rhetoric masked character rather than revealed, and this would present enormous challenges to the still maturing democracy, challenges that would ultimately be directed to the theatre to address.

THE LAW

The hallmark of the Athenian political and legal systems
was its amateurism. Most public officials, including those
who supervised the courts, were selected by lot and held
office for limited period, typically a year.... All significant policy decisions were debated and voted on in an
Assembly, where the quorum was 6,000 citizens, and all
significant legal cases were judged by bodies of 200 to
500 jurors or more.

     —Michael Gagarin, "Greek Oratory"

It is said that Drakon himself, when asked why he had
fixed the punishment of death for most offences, answered
that he considered these lesser crimes to deserve it, and
he had no greater punishment for more important ones.

     —Plutarch, *Plutarch's Lives*

Coinciding with a wish to arrive at an efficient and inclusive political
system was a desire to generate an effective legal instrument that once
applied, would transcend the chaos of vigilantism and tribal vendetta.
One of the earliest laws on record was devised by Draco who instituted
the sentence of exile for the crime of murder. His was the first written
constitution that Athenians ever had.

Here too, though, the act of writing, once introduced, altered the
landscape. Where before the law had been invested in an oral tradition
that only a select group of experts knew, interpreted, and imposed; the
new written laws were available to whoever wished to read, interpret,
and argue them. In fact, when a crime went to trial the most common
procedure was that the injured party brought suit against the accused.
The Athenians eagerly embraced this participatory approach to legal
recourse—some felt *too* eagerly embraced.

As the popularity of legal action grew, the intersection between persuasive rhetoric, sound legal procedure, and theatricality blurred and
was not always clear. Larger, more consequential legal cases were occasionally argued in the theatre, where more seats were available. The
speeches of those defending or prosecuting were delivered to whoever
attended and were considered, if not a form of theatre per se, a type of

vicarious entertainment. Some of the more notorious legal cases drew "full houses."

One indication of the popularity of this "courtroom drama" survives in the mention made in Aristophanes's satire of the legal system, *The Wasps*. In it, a character named Philocleon suffers from a mania for attending trials so insatiable that he dashes to the court immediately following his every evening meal, and is broken-hearted when he isn't permitted to sit in the front bench.

Aristophanes, who appeared before a court on a number of occasions himself and so knew whereof he spoke, commented upon and criticized the Athenian passion for litigation in his plays.

> ...Talk of lawsuits makes me sick.
> You know what I'd like?
> To smash the voting urns.[4]

If elements of the theatre could be found in the courts of Athens, it's equally remarkable how often issues, images, wording, and procedures of the courtroom emerged in the scripts of the Athenian theatre. In the manner in which characters argued their points and positioned their defences, it's evident that the boundaries between trial and theatrical performance were anything but clear. On occasion, trials and legal protocol were integrated in full measure into plays. In *The Eumenides*, the play culminates with a trial presided over by Athena, *The Wasps* contains images and content pertaining to the law, *The Acharnians* concludes with a mock trial, as does *The Frogs*. Whether the tone was satirical, as it was in *The Wasps*, or sombre as it was in the *Oresteia*, it's apparent that there was a deep-rooted, abiding interest in the mechanics of justice, and that the principle ideas of legal address had thoroughly percolated, simmered, and leeched into the dramaturgy of these early plays.

---

4   Aristophanes, *The Wasps* in *Aristophanes: The Complete Plays*, trans. Paul Roche (New York: New American Library, 2005), 263.

HISTORY

Prior to the development of the written word, history was an indistinguishable compilation of hearsay, legend, myth, gossip, folk wisdom, and occasionally, fact.

The works of Homer, based upon an oral tradition, are a prime example of this kind of murky prehistory that arbitrarily blended geographically identifiable locations with fictive locations and historical human beings alongside gods, demigods, and spirits. Written language changed that.

As the written word was more widely employed and read, an attempt was made to record events of the past with greater accuracy. Two individuals in particular have been credited with this new approach to history.

The first, Herodotus, is thought to have lived in the fifth century BCE. The dates most commonly used to bracket his life are 484–425 BCE. He was the first individual known to have attempted to distill, track, and describe events around a single historical event.

His book, entitled aptly, *The Histories*, documents the events leading up to and surrounding the conflict that would become known as the Greco-Persian Wars. As part of his research for the book, he travelled widely, noted events that he observed, and interviewed people he met. The resulting text was part travelogue, part journal, part objective reportage, and part reflective meditation that still contained—and was quite charming because it contained—stories, hearsay, and unsubstantiated anecdotes. In fact, his entire process was to a large measure "anecdotal" in that Herodotus passed along any information that he felt might shed light upon the issues he was investigating. "I am obliged," he said, "to record the things I am told, but I am certainly not required to believe them—this remark may be taken to apply to the whole of my account."[5]

Much of what historians know today of the ancient world is as a direct result of these early writings and the efforts of Herodotus. Because of his extensive work, and because of the (for its time) novel approach that Herodotus applied, he became known, at least from Roman times on, as the "Father of History."

Following shortly after Herodotus, however, another individual appeared who took a more objective, more dispassionate approach to the arrangement of time and events. This individual, Thucydides

---

5   Herodotus, *The Histories*, trans. Robin Wakefield (Oxford: Oxford University Press, 1998), 7:152.

A bust of Herodotus. Photograph taken at the Museum of the Ancient Agora of Athens, courtesy of the Hellenic Ministry of Culture.

(c.460–c.395 BCE), brought greater rigour to the discipline as he worked up a text that would consume the better part of his adult life and would eventually become the model for modern history. *The History of the Peloponnesian War*, his life project, relied less on anecdotal sources, instead attempting to present only those elements that could objectively be understood as facts.

Historians in times since have appreciated the pains he took to provide a more impartial view of circumstances. In his introductory chapter to Thucydides, John Finley wrote:

> ...the *History* [*of the Peloponnesian War*], virtually alone of Athenian writings, records analytically the creative workings of the first democracy, and, what is more, in a sympathetic spirit and from the point of view of an observer and pupil of events, not of a moralist or a censor.[6]

Consequently, while Herodotus may have become known as the Father of History, it was the course that Thucydides plotted that future historians later adopted.

The writings of these two gentlemen hold significance not just for the evidence that they assembled of the operations of a bygone time, but because they represented a pivotal point of departure from the world of myth. Thucydides predicted as much when he wrote:

> And it may well be that my history will seem less easy to read because of the absence in it of a romantic element. It will be enough for me, however, if these words of mine are judged useful by those who want to understand clearly the events which happened in the past and which (human nature being what it is) will, at some time or other and in much the same ways, be repeated in the future. My work is not a piece of writing designed to meet the taste of an immediate public, but was done to last forever.[7]

With greater focus being applied to separating fact-based history from the more malleable, culturally based notions of legend and lore, theatre was permitted to break new ground as well. In its plays it sought new points of access for the old myths, and deconstructed legends in ways that felt fresh, frightening, and terribly emotional. This was a new kind of storytelling that borrowed something from everyday observations of human behaviour, from historical as well as mythic accounts, and then tied it all to character, context, and the explosive, unpredictable outcomes of choice.

---

6   John H. Finley Jr., "Introduction," in *The Complete Writings of Thucydides: The Peloponnesian War by Thucydides*, trans. Richard Crawley (New York: Modern Library, 1951), ix.

7   Thucydides, *History of the Peloponnesian War*, trans. Rex Warner (London: Penguin Books, 1972), 1:20.

PHILOSOPHY

The Greek thinkers in the archaic and classical periods performed their wisdom in different ways in front of different audiences.

—Andrea Wilson Nightingale,
"Sages, Sophists, and Philosophers"

At the same time that theatre was beginning to find its form and democracy was establishing guidelines for procedure and due process, philosophy was attempting to more thoroughly engage with the world of thought, morality, spirit, and Self.

Plato is most often credited with initiating a systemic examination of ethical and metaphysical concerns that would become known to the world as philosophy, but this new study relied heavily upon the prior efforts of Socrates, whose work provided a theoretical foundation, and Aristotle, who later provided a language and methodology for further inquiry.

This new approach to thinking had an influence on many different levels of Athenian society, and it would be wrong to view the transmission of these ideas as something that occurred solely in a quiet or scholarly fashion. Andrea Nightingale aptly refers to Greek thinkers "performing" their wisdom. Many of the activities that the thinkers of the time engaged in look, to today's eyes, remarkably like performance. Public debates in the market or at the Lyceum attracted audiences who rooted for one side or the other. Winners were applauded, and losers derided.

All these elements of thought, and the manner in which they were transmitted, seeped into the theatre. In the works of Euripides it is possible to catch echoes of philosophy. In Aristophanes's *The Clouds* we have characters debate the merits of philosophy and imitate the jargon of philosophers.

In short, these novelties, these new institutions, these innovative solutions to the changing requirements of the Archaic age all left their fossil legacy, their thumbprints, upon the Greek theatre. The written word, the new separation of history and myth, the institutionalized sporting events, philosophy, and the rhetorical and legal arts of persuasion all provided a rich environment in which the institution of theatre matured until, as Aristotle put it in the *Poetics*: "After undergoing many transformations tragedy came to rest, because it had attained its natural state."[8]

---

8   Aristotle, *Poetics*, trans. Malcolm Heath (London: Penguin Books, 1996), 8.

PROCESS

4. LEARNING FROM THE EVOLUTION δ′

It's possible that certain crucial ingredients of contemporary drama may already have been present in the dithyrambs that existed prior to 530 BCE when Thespis introduced individual characters who spoke apart from, and responded to, the chorus. Certainly, though, from the time Aeschylus first drafted a play for production in 499 BCE, a dynamic process was initiated that resulted in the transformation of the theatre landscape.

Howsoever much of theatre existed earlier, this period of transformation was sufficient in scope that by 350 BCE, Aristotle felt able to draft a series of penetrating notes for his lectures, establishing a guideline for dramaturgical critique based on a very specific aesthetic code of conduct.

It was within the crucible of those nearly two hundred and fifty turbulent years that the template for contemporary Western theatre was set. During this time theatre transformed from ritual—which contained and transmitted its own coded and complex narratives—to a new paradigm relying upon conflict, causality, and consequence. Aristotle is uncompromising in his assessment. "Tragedy," he tells us, "advanced by slow degrees; each new element... in turn developed. Having passed through many changes, it found its natural form, and there it stopped."[1]

Of course, from our privileged point on the inclining slope of history, it's possible to consider the past with greater objectivity and know that theatre didn't stop developing, but continued to evolve. Elements of greater and lesser consequence continued to be introduced—*but* the rate of change and the scope of change were sufficiently arrested that one can present the plays of two thousand years ago on the contemporary stage and still elicit an emotional and empathic response from an audience.

The two key questions that spring from this metamorphosis are as follows. First, in the midst of all this ferment and change, with the political, judicial, philosophical, and literary environments shifting and colliding against one another, what primary force thrust the theatre into its new incarnation?

---

1   Aristotle, *Poetics*, 8.

Secondly, why did it stop? If the change was merely part of a continuing evolution, couldn't it be anticipated that theatre would continue to adjust in a similar manner over the subsequent millennia? Unless the change addressed so profound a need that the template, once fired in the kiln of the turbulent two hundred and fifty years, was set for perpetuity.

EARLY INFLUENCES AND PARALLEL TRAJECTORIES

THE OLYMPICS

Let's return to the Olympics for a moment. As has already been noted, there are certain parallels presented by the developments of drama and the Olympics. Both began as religious rites. Both were competitions. Like drama, the Olympic events were held in outdoor forums. Both separated spectators from participants within formally segregated areas—a space for those "performing" and a separate space for "spectators." One can perceive remarkably similar activities in both instances; the participants engaging in a series of demanding struggles that the seated spectators observed and responded to.

The stadium at Delphi.

The theatre at Delphi.

In the same way that drama experienced a gradual series of cumulative changes, the Olympics evolved from that one simple foot race into a far more complex affair involving many activities.

Although it wasn't established with this end in mind, one of the outcomes of the Olympics was that the spectators were enabled to determine the pre-eminent athletic worthiness of a single participant from within a wide field of capable contestants. Athletes would vie in their separate events and, ultimately, the *most* worthy was crowned with laurels. To spectators, a group of athletes might all seem equally worthy initially, but the mechanism of the competition would conduct a kind of highly discriminating screening that would select only those who were *most* worthy.

So, in a sense, the Olympics may be viewed as a *mechanism that permitted discernment*. Discernment to what end, however? What could be the purpose of such a mechanism?

It's clear that to the Greeks of that time the Olympics weren't an amusement or entertainment, but rather were a very serious, very sacred event. From the day of commencement until the games were concluded an international truce applied to all participants, and a certain heightened code of conduct was adhered to. To be awarded the designation of an Olympian meant much more than simply being able to demonstrate certain physical abilities. Alongside physical prowess, an Olympian was expected to exhibit attributes of character.

Herodotus makes special reference to those who had won Olympic honours in the past. His reference in Book 8, Chapter 26 makes explicit the connection between "character" and the athleticism of the Games.

In this chapter, the invading Persian, Tritantaechmus learns that contestants will receive only a garland of olive leaves as a prize for winning and, astonished, blurts out, "Well, Mardonius, what sort of men are these you have brought us to fight? They make excellence rather than money the reason for a contest."[2]

The connection of Olympian success to leadership characteristics is further underscored in Chapter 33 of Book 9. In this chapter, Tisamenus receives a prediction from the Oracle at Delphi that he will win five crucial contests. Herodotus notes that Tisamenus specialized in the pentathlon event at the Olympics and had only missed winning previously by one event. It is intimated that partially in acknowledgement of this honour he is recruited by the Lacedaemonians to be a war-leader. And there are further suggestions that to be an Olympian is to be regarded as especially worthy—again Herodotus references the participation of King Alexander I in the 496 BCE Olympics and implies that it at least partially proved his citizenship and connection to Greece.

The flamboyant and erratic leader Alcibiades offered this telling comment regarding his participation at the Olympic Games as he attempted to persuade the Athenians that the campaign against Sicily should be mounted. Note how he introduces his theme:

> I must begin by saying that I have a better right than others to hold the command, and that I think I am quite worthy of the position.... There was a time when the Hellenes imagined that our city had been ruined by the war, but they came to consider it even greater than it really is, because of the splendid show I made as its representative at the Olympic games, when I entered seven chariots for the chariot race (more than any private individual has entered before) and I took the first, second, and fourth places, and saw that everything else was arranged in a style worthy of my victory. It is customary for such things

---

2   Herodotus, *The Histories*, 8:26.

to bring honour, and the fact that they are done at all must also give an impression of power.[3]

Here we see an individual using the Olympic Games as an instrument to definitively prove his leadership worthiness. The Olympics, then, could be understood as having been considered helpful for detecting elements of character that might have been perceived as useful to a leader. And one can recognize that physical prowess—speed, strength, stamina—and the concomitant abilities to ignore pain, to function under pressure, to focus upon the task at hand even while under intense scrutiny, might very well be useful to a leader of some martial endeavour.

But as regards discerning other necessary leadership skills that are required during peacetime—say honesty, integrity, diligence, and intelligence—the Olympics had their limitations. As Greek society evolved and required of its citizens the ability to select individuals upon the basis of these other criteria, other mechanisms would have to be invented to test for another skill set.

---

3   Thucydides, *History of the Peloponnesian War*, 6:16.

THE DEVELOPMENT OF DEMOCRACY

From the time Solon first applied his democratic reforms to the Athenian political system, it is impossible to examine ancient literature without sensing a ripple of both anxiety and excitement. Discussion of the democratic movement surfaced in the likeliest and unlikeliest of places.

In Book 3, following the description of a daring, bloody court coup, Herodotus devoted a number of pages to an impossibly long debate between co-conspirators, Ottanes, Megabyzus, and Darius, regarding the benefits and drawbacks of three prominent forms of governance: democracy, oligarchy, and monarchy. In his historical chronicle each political form is provided with a proponent who describes and lobbies upon its behalf. Ottanes breezily dismisses monarchies:

> Make a man a monarch, and even if he is the most moral person in the world, he will leave his customary way of thinking.... He resents the existence of the best men, while the worst of them make him happy. There is no one better than him at welcoming slander, and there is no one more erratic in his behavior. I mean, if your admiration for him is moderate, he is offended at your lack of total subservience, and if you are totally subservient, he is angry at you as a flatterer. And now I come to the most important problems with monarchy. A monarch subverts a country's ancestral customs, takes women against their will, and kills men without trial. What about majority rule, on the other hand? In the first place, it has the best of all names to describe it—equality before the law. In the second place, it is entirely free of the vices of monarchy. It is government by lot, it is accountable government, and it refers all decisions to the common people. [4]

Megabyzus dismisses the notion of putting power in the hands of ignorant masses. "...[K]nowledge and the masses are incompatible," he insists. "How could anyone know what is right without having been taught it or having an innate awareness of it? No, the approach of the general populace is that of a river swollen with winter rain: they rush

---

4   Herodotus, *The Histories*, 3:80.

blindly forward and sweep things before them."[5] Instead, he offers oligarchy as the only sensible choice of government.

Finally, Darius speaks, and he points out that oligarchy inevitably leads to:

> personal feuds... because every one of them wants to come out on top and have his own views prevail. This leads them to become violently antagonistic toward one another, so the factions arise, which leads to bloodshed, which leads ultimately to monarchy—which just goes to show that it is by far the best system.[6]

Darius of course, is advancing his own agenda; plotting, as he is, to make himself monarch.

It's an astonishing conversation. Astonishing for its placement, occurring as it does hot on the heels of a variety of beheadings and mayhem, astonishing for the length that Herodotus devotes to it, and astonishing for its penetrating assessment of the comparative strengths and liabilities of these political forms. Although it seems unlikely that as complete a record of so essentially a private conversation could possibly have existed, Herodotus assured his readers that this conversation did, in fact, occur. Putting that aside, however, what can be discerned from this exchange is that deliberations and discussions regarding issues of governance were going on in many places in the regions bordering the Mediterranean, and over an extended period of time.

An analysis of a similar kind is also revealed decades later in the writings of Thucydides, through the filter of Pericles's moving Funeral Oration, in which the many benefits of the democratic system are extolled.

> Let me say that our system of government does not copy the institutions of our neighbours. It is more the case of our being a model to others.... When it is a question of settling private disputes, everyone is equal before the law, when it is a question of putting one person before another in positions of public responsibility, what counts is not membership of a particular class, but the actual ability which the person possesses. No one, so long as he has

---

5   Ibid.
6   Ibid., 3:82.

it in him to be of service to the state, is kept in political obscurity because of poverty. And, just as our political life is free and open, so is our day-to-day life...[7]

Aristotle devotes space in *Politics* to comparing and contrasting the forms of government, noting that "[t]he real difference between democracy and oligarchy is poverty and wealth. Wherever men rule by reason of their wealth, whether they be few or many, that is an oligarchy, and where the poor rule, that is democracy" before dismissing democracy as a system that privileges the needy and the indigent.[8]

It is perhaps, on second thought, entirely understandable that this kind of debate should have filtered through literature, given the high stakes. Democracy, while presenting a tempting option, demanded a great deal from the people, unused as they were to actively participating in their own governance.

One of the greatest challenges of a democracy may be said to lie in the ability of the voting constituents to discern. After all, as Darius rightly pointed out, a tyrant is in most respects free from influence. He is not chosen by the people, but rather the tyrant *imposes his choice* upon his subjects. In this kind of autocratic society, the ability of the masses to discern the inner attributes of individuals is relatively unimportant.

Democracy, however, works a little differently and requires a different skill set of its constituent members. A democracy requires that the people arrive at some kind of mutually agreed upon understanding concerning the abilities and strengths of individuals entrusted with collective responsibilities. The

A bust of Pericles. Photograph presented with the permission of the British Museum.

7   Thucydides, *History of the Peloponnesian War*, 145.
8   Aristotle, *The Politics and The Constitution of Athens*, trans. Stephen Everson (Cambridge: Cambridge University Press, 1996), 72.

people must first be able to agree upon the criteria necessary to choose individuals entrusted with leadership tasks, and then develop the ability to determine which individuals best manifest these criteria. When Pericles observed during his Funeral Oration that in Athens "...when it is a question of putting one person before another in positions of public responsibility, what counts is not membership of a particular class, but the actual ability that the man possesses." he was referring to that precise process of identifying those particular individual traits and then recruiting and inducting the individual to a position of leadership.[9]

But attributes like trustworthiness, intelligence, and courage are difficult to assess. These talents, such as they are, remain largely veiled. Likewise, character flaws and weaknesses can be hidden and concealed relatively easily—and it may be as important to detect these flaws as it is to detect the strengths.

To make things more complicated, while it may be possible to judge a person worthy in their day-to-day existence, it is entirely possible that an individual will prove worthy in the quotidian matters of their life, and yet less than worthy under difficult and demanding circumstances. And it is precisely under difficult and demanding circumstances that leadership skills are most required. (As I write this it is curious to hear this very paradox articulated in almost exactly this wording, within the context of the most recent American presidential election. Presidential candidate Senator John McCain, as a veteran of the Vietnam War and a former prisoner of war, maintains that he has already undergone trials that have exposed his leadership skills. Senator McCain asserts, however, that the Democratic contender, Senator Barack Obama, has "Not been tested.")

These challenges, and the questions that arose from them, were turned over again and again by the best thinkers of the time. Thucydides attempted to calculate the precise importance of character as it related to leadership in his description of Pericles:

> Pericles, because of his position, his intelligence, and his known integrity, could respect the liberty of the people and at the same time hold them in check. It was he who led them, rather than they who led him ... so in what was nominally a democracy, power was really in the hands of the first citizen.[10]

---

9   Ibid., 145.
10   Ibid., 164.

THE EMPLOYMENT OF RHETORIC

The incline Athenians laboured up from autocratic rule to participatory democracy was along a very steep gradient. Just consider the smallest portion of it for a moment. The tyrant Draco made a primitive attempt to establish a judicial system. Civil disturbances erupted. Solon reformed the constitution. His constitution was subverted and suppressed by Pisistratus. Pisistratus gained power, lost power, gained it again—and died. His sons Hippias and Hipparchus assumed power until Hipparchus was assassinated. Then Hippias arrested the assassins, suppressed the uprising, and governed on his own. Discontent rose once again until, having solicited the secret assistance of conspiring Spartan troops, Cleisthenes seized the reins of government and instituted democratic reform.

It's been said that people must develop certain social skills to successfully navigate a democracy. One thing that is evident from this chaos: initially the Greeks did not possess those skills.

But they *began* to develop them. Their famed rhetorical schools were one way in which Athenians attempted to build the democratic muscles their population needed to engage more fully in the political process, to persuade, to conciliate, to gather consensus.

Aristotle was very interested in rhetoric, and thought it linked to an understanding of the character of the speaker.

> Of the modes of persuasion furnished by the spoken word there are three kinds. The first kind depends on the personal character of the speaker; the second on putting the audience into a certain frame of mind; the third on the proof, or apparent proof, provided by the words of the speech itself. Persuasion is achieved by the speaker's personal character when the speech is so spoken as to make us think him credible. We believe good men more fully and more readily than others: this is true generally whatever the question is, and absolutely true where exact certainty is impossible and opinions are divided. This kind of persuasion, like the others, should be achieved by what the speaker says, not by what people think of his character before he begins to speak. It is not true, as some writers assume in their treatises on rhetoric, that the personal

goodness revealed by the speaker contributes nothing to his power of persuasion; on the contrary, his character may almost be called the most effective means of persuasion he possesses.[11]

As individuals exercised their oratorical abilities and participated fully in their government, the polis of Athens produced some of the finest speeches in recorded history. Many of those speeches have survived into our times, and are admired and studied today.

But the Athenians simultaneously discovered that an individual could speak skilfully, soulfully, persuasively—and still be wrong. Worse, an individual could apply these same rhetorical skills to distort issues, to enflame passions, and to deceive others. So, in a society that required that its citizens agree upon decisions, rhetorical skills could be seen, at best, as a deeply flawed mechanism, and at worst as exacerbating an already complicated situation.

One case illustrates the great risk that the state ran when it relied upon rhetoric.

Alcibiades, a contemporary of Pericles and Sophocles, was a fine speaker, well-educated, and connected to one of the oldest and most respected families in Athens.

This critical speech, delivered by him to the Athenians as they deliberated over whether to attack Sicily, was instrumental in persuading the Athenians that the risks inherent in the proposed invasion were not as great as they thought.

> …This is the way we won our empire and this is the way all empires have been won—by coming vigorously to the help of all who ask for it, irrespective of whether they are Hellenes or not. Certainly if everyone were to remain inactive or go in for racial distinctions when it is a question of giving assistance, we should add very little to our empire, and we should be more likely to risk losing it altogether. One does not only defend oneself against a superior power when one is attacked; one takes measures in advance to prevent the attack materializing. And it is not possible for us to calculate, like housekeepers, exactly how much empire we want to have. The fact is that we

---

11   Aristotle, *Aristotle's Rhetoric*, trans. W. Rhys Roberts, The Internet Classics Archive, http://classics.mit.edu/Aristotle/rhetoric.html (accessed May 7, 2009).

have reached a stage where we are forced to plan new conquests and forced to hold on to what we have got, because there is a danger that we ourselves may fall under the power of others unless others are in our power.[12]

During and following the Sicilian Campaign of the Peloponnesian War, Alcibiades proved himself to be almost pathologically untrustworthy. He switched sides so many times between the Spartans and the Athenians that it is difficult to determine whose side he ever truly believed he was on, except of course his own. And the Sicilian Campaign, quite to the contrary of his claim, was not the way that empires were won. Instead the campaign resulted in an unparalleled defeat and had disastrous consequences for Athens.

So the Greeks had a growing awareness that rhetoric, while it could be a very effective instrument of persuasion, was a flawed device for understanding character. In fact, it could serve a completely opposite function. It could become a mechanism for obscuring and distorting truth of character.

---

12   Thucydides, *History of the Peloponnesian War*, 421.

THE RIGHT TOOLS FOR THE RIGHT OPERATION

Over two millennia after Sophocles penned *Oedipus* and *Antigone*, and Aeschylus, *Agamemnon*; Nietzsche wrote "The Athenian went to the theatre in order to hear beautiful speeches."[13]

He was only half right.

Where Nietzsche got it wrong was in the matter of "intent." The Greeks didn't attend the theatre to just listen to beautiful speeches, they went to get inoculated.

After all, if rhetoric could mask, if rhetoric could conceal, what was a mechanism for *unmasking*? What instrument might be developed to discern these inner attributes? And because it was necessary that there be some agreement among the population as to which leadership skills were important, how might consensus be reached across a broad population concerning which skills were *most* essential? For answers to these questions the Greeks turned to the theatre.

The theatre permitted the adult population to sit together, to observe individuals on stage undergo situations of extreme stress, and then encouraged the audience to arrive at a consensus regarding the failings or successes of those characters on stage. The public observance of these dramatized struggles might, in one way, be viewed as a training ground for the maturing democratic constituents.

For a democracy to function properly, it's not sufficient for the *administration* to change—the *public* itself must go through something of a transformation. The public must learn to operate from a new, but commonly held set of assumptions. The theatre encouraged and facilitated the development of that collective skill set.

The audience, as they observed a play whose central storyline most often examined matters pertaining to leadership and governance, could also simultaneously observe their fellow audience members. Where there was consensus in emotional response among the audience to a storyline, an individual audience member might rightly intuit that there was consensus regarding an approach to governance. In this scenario the audience's observations of the action on stage, and the audience's observations of the audience would be of equal importance.

Our modernized culture has witnessed the development of a number of arenas where the concept of "virtual training" has proven very useful.

---

13   F.W. Nietzsche, *The Gay Science*, trans. Walter Kaufmann (New York: Vantage Books, 1974), 80.

Where education has been found to be too expensive, too complex, or too dangerous, it has been possible to create electronic and web-based forums where skills can be practised and mastered with far less cost or risk. So today one can train to be a pilot of an airplane, virtually, without—at least initially—actually piloting an airplane. One can drive a car virtually, and learn the basics of road safety and vehicle manipulation, without initially risking the lives of actual pedestrians.

Drama, viewed this way, can be seen as an opportunity to "virtually" test drive the leadership determination skills of a population. From the safety of their seats they may detect the necessary attributes of leadership without incurring the risks and dangers associated with making a genuinely wrong choice. And there were, of course, very real and very costly risks associated with choosing wrong leaders.

Thucydides describes some of the high risks that accompanied a failure of leadership in his *History of the Peloponnesian Wars*:

> The leaders in the cities, each provided with the fairest profes-
> sions, on the one side with the cry of political equality of the
> people, on the other of a moderate aristocracy, sought prizes
> for themselves in those public interests which pretended to
> cherish, and recoiling from no means in their struggles for
> ascendancy, engaged in the direct excesses; in their acts of
> vengeance they went to even greater lengths, not stopping at
> what justice or the good of the state demanded...[14]

As a result of this failure of leadership we are told "every form of iniquity took root in the Hellenic countries."[15]

The manner in which theatre adapted to fill this particular niche would by no means have been explicit. A culture often responds to and acts upon the requirements of its time, without recognizing or articulating those needs to itself. In retrospect, for example, it is possible to see that evolution of urban civilizations responded to the development of large-scale agrarian initiatives and the ability to accumulate wealth—but these modifications of society were neither calculated nor explicitly articulated by or to its participants.

However, if in fact drama was evolving in response to a need to better understand character, particularly as character was manifested in a leadership role, one should be able to witness the evolution of the instruments of measurement and detection that served this particular need.

---

14   Ibid., 3:9.
15   Ibid.

SERVING A PARTICULAR NEED

Drama and tragedy experienced just such an evolution, with the development extending to several diverse ingredients.

As has already been determined, the number of individual roles appearing in plays was increased; first as modified by Thespis, then again by Aeschylus, and then once again by Sophocles. Storylines became increasingly complex—the plays of Aeschylus were more admired for the poetry of the speech, whereas the later plays of Sophocles and then Euripides were admired for the sophistication of the narrative. As the role of the chorus diminished and dialogue between characters took on greater significance, the metre of the dialogue changed to reflect the central place it would have in plays.

What were the results of these changes?

The increased number of individual actors, and the diminished role of the chorus allowed individual decision-making skills to be isolated and examined.

That the plots became more complex allowed the central struggle to be intensified, and the nuances and details of that struggle to be highlighted and examined more fully.

That the metre changed allowed for a less ritualized approach to language to be employed, which would in turn permit critical and timely matters of the day to be examined in the idiom of the day.

In other words, the mechanisms of the theatre were altered so that instead of simply evoking a celebrated ritual, the purpose was turned to investigating the *will of the protagonist* as it was exposed in the context of struggle. In this manner the decisions made by the protagonist might be better tested, illuminated, and presented for scrutiny.

If one sees the beginning of these modifications as receiving their first impulse with Pisistratus's introduction of drama at the Greater Dionysia and the introduction by Thespis of the individualized character role, then this evolution also coincides very closely with the democratic reforms introduced by Solon at the turn of the sixth century.

What sorts of individuals were featured in these tragedies? Even a quick overview of the plays that have survived to present times inform the reader that the narratives of the Greeks were overwhelmingly concerned with the critical decisions of kings, queens, and military leaders. This might have been predicted if one were to assume that the central concern of drama was to investigate and better understand the skills of leadership.

Oedipus Tyrannus by Sophocles places a king in a position of struggle and stress, during a plague—very much like the plague that Athens had experienced at the beginning of the Peloponnesian War—and then asks that the audience evaluate his leadership abilities. *The Persians* by Aeschylus follows this paradigm very closely as well. The leader, Xerxes in this case, is placed in a situation of stress—that of a major battle in a sweeping military campaign—and ultimately under the scrutiny of his mother, his people, and the even the ghost of his father, his skills of leadership are found wanting. Consider these lines from *The Persians*:

> All Asia weeps, bereft,
> Stripped of her men
> Xerxes took them
> Xerxes killed them.[16]

If Xerxes's decisions represented a failure of leadership, in what skills was he found wanting? The play concludes that inexperience, pridefulness, and bad consul resulting from keeping "...bad company..." were the qualities that led to his ultimate ruin.[17]

In *Seven Against Thebes*, Aeschylus again throws the spotlight squarely on matters of governance and leadership.

> What have you done here with your
> mad storming about but
> drained the people's hearts of
> courage and given cowardice
> a foothold?
> While the enemy successfully attacks us
> outside the walls, you destroy us from
> within!
> It's the price we pay for living with women!
> I will be obeyed!
> I demand strict obedience!
> And anyone, anyone, man or
> woman, who refuses my
> authority will have a judgement of
> death passed against him and be

---

16   Aeschylus, *The Persians*, in *Aeschylus: Plays One*, trans. Frederic Raphael and Kenneth McLeish (London: Methuen Drama, 1991), 18.

17   Aeschylus, *The Persians*, in *Aeschylus: The Complete Plays*, Vol. 2, trans. Carl R. Mueller (Hanover: A Smith and Kraus Books, 2002), 159.

stoned to death in the public
square! [18]

An individual—in this case Eteocles, the ruler of Thebes—is plunged
into a crisis as an attack on his city commences.

In that moment, as the enemy storms the walls, the audience is presented with an opportunity to examine precisely what one should do in
such a situation. It is significant that what is demonstrated is not just how
Eteocles comports *himself* in this trying situation, but how he guides
others. He has strong words of advice for those around him about what
actions they should take and the way they should compose themselves.

It is also worth recollecting that violence, skirmishing, and war were
not uncommon situations at that time. These would be the situations
that would demand the most of leaders, and so it would be essential that
a leader be able to conduct himself appropriately.

Interestingly, although comedy is often perceived to be different
from tragedy, and originating from a different impulse, when one examines the themes that the plays of the Old Comedy embraced, it appears
to share remarkable similarities with tragedy. The comedic plays, *The
Acharnians*, *The Knights*, and *Peace*, are explicitly about governance
and the attributes individuals bring to governance in times of turmoil.

In *The Knights*, a political satire, Aristophanes has two servants
vie for the attention of their master Demos—or, roughly translated, the
people—each claiming that they will serve him best. As part of the competition to show how he will be the better servant/political leader, the
character of the Sausage-Seller confronts the utterly corrupt Paphlagon.

PAPHLAGON
To hear you slinging mud like this is really distressing,
After all the things I've done for Demos and the
    Athenians—
Far more indeed than Themistocles did in his time for
    the city.

SAUSAGE-SELLER
City of Argos! Do you hear what he says? What colossal
    Brass!
Do you dare compare your lousy self with Themistocles?

---

18   Aeschylus, *Seven Against Thebes*, in *Aeschylus: The Complete Plays*, *Vol. 2*,
trans. Carl R. Mueller (Hanover: A Smith and Kraus Books, 2002), 192–193.

—Who finding the city like a half-empty wine-cup filled it
Right to the brim; Themistocles, who grafted the
  Piraeus
On to it like a tidbit, adding new fish to our menu
but losing none of the old. And what's *your*
  contribution?
Partition walls that diminish the city and make the
  Athenians
appear provincial and petty—that; and *oracles*—I ask
  you!
And you dare compare your lazy lousy self with
  Themistocles!
And he went into exile and you stay, wiping your fingers
  on the best bread.[19]

A later comedic play by Aristophanes, *Lysistrata*, is of even greater interest as regards issues of governance and leadership. At the opening of this play Sparta and Athens are in a state of war, which their political leaders are either unable or unwilling to end. The play takes a decidedly democratic stance when it has its citizens look elsewhere for guidance—to their women.

Frustrated by the lack of meaningful negotiations between the warring cities, Lysistrata, the determined female protagonist of the play, seizes the initiative to end the war. She organizes the women of both Sparta and Athens to take political action, and endeavours to compel those individuals in positions of political power to see reason.

MAGISTRATE
And how, pray, would you propose to restore peace and
order in all the countries of Greece?

LYSISTRATA
It's the easiest thing in the world!

MAGISTRATE
Come, tell us how; I am curious to know.

---

19   Aristophanes, *The Knights*, in *Aristophanes, Plays One*, trans. Patric Dickinson (Oxford: Oxford University Press, 1970), 82.

LYSISTRATA
When we are winding thread, and it is tangled, we pass
the spool across and through the skein, now this way,
now that way; even so, to finish of the war, we shall
send embassies hither and thither and everywhere, to
disentangle matters.

MAGISTRATE
And is it with your yarn, and your skeins, and your
spools, you think to appease so many bitter enmities,
you silly women?

LYSISTRATA
If only you had common sense, you would always do in
politics the same as we do with our yarn.

MAGISTRATE
Come, how is that, eh?

LYSISTRATA
First we wash the yarn to separate the grease and filth;
do the same with all bad citizens, sort them out and
drive them forth with rods—they're the refuse of the
city. Then for all such as come crowding up in search
of employments and offices, we must card them thoroughly; then, to bring them all to the same standard,
pitch them pell-mell into the same basket, resident aliens
or no, allies, debtors to the State, all mixed up together.
Then as for our Colonies, you must think of them as
so many isolated hanks; find the ends of the separate
threads, draw them to a centre here, wind them into
one, make one great hank of the lot, out of which the
public can weave itself a good, stout tunic.[20]

Written in 411 BCE, long after Thespis supposedly introduced the
first actor, this play is a fascinating indication of how far theatre had
advanced. The play not only tests Lysistrata as a leader, and through
her actions models behaviours that it suggests would be more appropri-

---

20   Aristophanes, *Lysistrata*, trans. Anonymous, Greek Texts, http://www.greek-
texts.com/library/Aristophanes/Lysistrata/eng/index.html (accessed May 7, 2009).

ate for leaders to manifest, but it also hints that it may be necessary for Athenians to recruit leaders from other demographics, and perhaps other genders.

The value of theatre's "virtual experience" becomes evident here. This imagined political act/manifesto-for-peace could happen nowhere else! In this courageous play, not only are the leaders of the time condemned and found wanting in terms of imagination and determination—a dangerous criticism given the temper of the times—but the play offers a radical solution. It suggests that women might possess wisdom and leadership abilities that went largely unrecognized in Greek society. This would have been an especially daring suggestion if, as has been suggested by some, women were not even permitted to attend performances.

Aeschylus's tragic trilogy, *The Oresteia*, on the other hand, examines leadership decisions as they related to civic governance. When Agamemnon, King of Argos, returns home at the beginning of the initial play, the Trojan War has ended. These three related plays, *Agamemnon*, *The Libation Bearers*, and *The Eumenides*, instead concern themselves with how one can live correctly and govern justly.

In this final passage of *The Eumenides*, the exploration of governance and justice is clear.

Orestes, having slain his mother for her murder of his father, is in turn pursued by the vengeful, implacable Furies. There being no place to escape the determined demigods, he at last seeks refuge with Athena who, modelling leadership rather than simply rendering a judgment and enforcing her will, convenes a trial of twelve Athenians. At the conclusion of the trial, Athena addresses the judges and advises them.

ATHENA
Pass to each free man's heart, by day and night
Enjoining, Thou shalt do no unjust thing,
So long as law stands as it stood of old
Unmarred by civic change. Look you, the spring
Is pure, but foul it once with influx vile
And muddy clay, and none can drink thereof.
Therefore, O citizens, I bid ye bow
In awe to this command, Let no man live
Uncurbed by law nor curbed by tyranny;
Nor banish ye the monarchy of Awe
Beyond the walls; untouched by fear divine,
No man doth justice in the world of men
Therefore in purity and holy dread

Stand and revere; so shall ye have and hold
A saying bulwark of the state and land,
Such as no man hath ever elsewhere known,
Nor in far Scythia, nor in Pelops' realm.
Thus I ordain it now, a council-court
Pure and unsullied by the lust of gain,
Sacred and swift to vengeance, wakeful ever
To champion men who sleep, the country's guard.
Thus have I spoken, thus to mine own clan
Commended it for ever. Ye who judge,
Arise, take each his vote, mete out the right,
Your oath revering. Lo, my word is said.[21]

"Thou shalt do no unjust thing," is how Athena finally admonishes the jury, and by extension the audience attending the theatre. How does a leader govern justly? How does a culture develop a common frame of reference so that they may respond to questions of this nature? It is entirely significant in this case that a goddess with infinite power is shown *choosing* to consult with a jury about issues of justice, and that instead of leaving the Furies unsatisfied at their lost case, she instead elects to negotiate a fair compromise with them. Even the gods, the play seems to suggest, cannot govern without consensus of the governed.

These questions of leadership, posed in the theatre and meditated upon by the attending audience, were critical. Failure to determine the correct skills, and the corresponding inability to choose wise leaders, could have lasting deleterious impact upon a society.

The theatre wasn't the only instrument that the Greeks had at their disposal to investigate questions of character and leadership but by the time Euripides was writing, it had certainly evolved into an instrument of some weight and substance.

In the theatre, a member of the audience might practise decision-making skills through forecasting the play's outcome, might argue with the playwright's thesis, might agree or disagree with others regarding the choices of the portrayed leader, and then exit equipped with a richer experience to draw upon. In the real world the consequences of bad decision-making could literally shatter a society.

This, then, was the modified instrument that the Greeks passed on to the Romans, and through the Romans, to Western culture.

---

21   Aeschylus, *The Eumenides*, trans. E.D.A. Morshead, The Internet Classics Archive, http://classics.mit.edu/Aeschylus/eumendides.html (accessed May 7, 2009).

ALIENATION IN THE CONTEMPORARY THEATRE

Participants in the modern theatre often misunderstand this development of playwriting. It is not uncommon to read references to a "confining structure" or that the "the classic structure may be too constraining."

This view is summed up by authors William Missouri Downs and Lou Anne Wright in the following quotation: "[T]he dominance of story over character is not new. In the long history of the theatre, character usually holds a backseat to story. Aristotle... in *Poetics* said character takes second place. In the modern theatre, we like to think character is more important..."[22]

In browsing playwriting texts it's not unusual to come upon phrases describing something as a "character-based playwriting" process, as opposed to a process based upon sound structure or strength of story. There is a general feeling of resistance to what is seen as "old-fashioned Aristotelian drama"—as though Aristotle had invented the form, or held a patent upon it.

The public today, bombarded as it is by stories in film, television, and the electronic media that often seem derivative, contrived, stereotypical, and blatantly recycled, is justly cynical as regards structure. The weary audience cannot be blamed if it begins to associate structure with a mechanical, formulaic approach to storytelling.

At the same time, among contemporary academics, a postmodern sensibility has challenged core notions of identity and authorial objectivity. Identity, according to postmodern theory, is a mirage, with individuals assumed to possess and shed many identities over a lifetime. There is an accompanying sense of skepticism that any author would be able to objectively create the precise conditions capable of assessing character and identity, even if such things actually existed.

Nevertheless, although social conventions like identity and character may be regarded as constructs in an abstract and theoretical sense, they are lived and experienced in a very real sense. An individual does not wake in the morning and ask, "Who am I?" or "Who have I been made today?" The individual assumes that some essential *someone* lives within their skin, and that same essential *someone* wakes, works, breathes, eats, and conducts daily life guided by that core identity.

---

22   William M. Downs and Lou Anne Wright, *Playwriting From Formula to Form: A Guide to Writing a Play* (Fort Worth, TX: Harcourt Brace College Publishers, 1998), 18.

Likewise, when an individual is introduced to a stranger, the conventional introduction means something genuine. A person does not inquire of a stranger, "Tell me who you think you are at this given moment," or "What, of the many identities culture and history have fashioned for you, do you believe you could share with me?" They wish to know exactly and precisely *who* that one person is, and they believe that the information is deliverable and that the information holds meaning.

And this offers us a glimpse at the sustaining value of the theatre as it has been passed down from the Greeks, and in part explains the enduring popularity of a narrative-based theatre, in an age that has grown a little gun-shy of story. It is utilitarian. The theatre is based upon the idea that the world is knowable and that the information that one receives from one's senses is useful. It is based upon an understanding that actions in a real world have genuine consequences. But more than anything else, it is based upon two complementary essential notions. That *someone* inhabits a body, and that this someone lives in a *real world*.

Between these two essential notions an equation is formulated that calculates identity—or character in this case—as a quantity that exists in a real and knowable world, and then attempts to appraise that quantity within the context of conflicting forces in an objective universe.

A good deal has changed since Thespis introduced a new kind of tragedy to the Festival of Dionysus in the sixth century BCE. The world of the ancient Greeks is not the same one we live in today. The democratic impulses that vexed and ultimately transformed Greek culture have continued to play out in our culture in different ways. There is greater freedom and individuation afforded citizens in our culture, and consequently audiences attending the theatre are less interested in, or tolerant of, viewing stories that are solely framed around the dilemmas of political or military leaders. But the crises that we experience feel real to us and continue to call out for our attention. The people that share our lives don't feel like abstractions, they feel genuine, and we genuinely yearn to understand them. And the theatre continues to offer itself as a potent instrument to facilitate that understanding.

The theatre that has been passed down to us is one that meshes character with story. The dramatic form that comprises today's theatre evolved, not to ignore character, but rather to explore character, and contemporary playwrights who disregard the inherent capacities of struggle and conflict forfeit the principle mechanism designed for investigating and comprehending human behaviour.

LEGACY

In addition to appreciating the development of the theatrical mechanism for what it has become and what it can accomplish, it is important that playwrights acknowledge the elements of writing that the Greeks executed especially well.

There are five ingredients that bear individual attention: Character, Economy, Contrast, Authority, and Transformation.

5. CHARACTER ε′

What human beings need is some clear index
of who is a friend and who is not—
a diagnostic of soul—
and every man should have two voices,
one righteous and the other however it happens to be,
so that the righteous voice could refute the unrighteous
and we would not be duped.
—Theseus from *Hippolytus* by Euripides

Pisistratus appeared to pay more attention to him than the others, for he was crafty and pleasant of speech, a protector of the poor, and a man of moderation even in his quarrels. The qualities which he had not, he affected to possess, giving himself out to be a cautious and law-abiding man, who loved even-handed justice and was enraged at any revolutionary proceedings. Thus he deceived the people; but Solon soon saw through him, and detected his plans before anyone else...
—Plutarch, *Plutarch's Lives*

The Greek theatre understood that plot and character were not simply connected, but were literally two faces of the same coin. The Greeks excelled, at least partially, in the careful selection of the *particular* struggle that most tested a character. These struggles were rarely minor. The forces that confronted the protagonists of Greek drama may have been human, but they often represented other much larger forces: the might of the government, the will of the gods, destiny. It was understood that character was best revealed and the audience brought to greatest intimacy and knowledge of the character when the struggle had a certain size and scale.

What the Greek theatre on occasion lacked in subtlety, it more than made up in power and lasting impact. There are a number of characters who have survived to modern times because their struggles were of such scorching intensity that they were seared in the heat and rendered luminous.

MEDEA
BY EURIPIDES

In this celebrated play, Euripides presents the legendary, larger-than-life anti-hero, Medea. This spurned wife is volatile, violent, and monstrous in the actions she chooses—and yet she is still not wholly unsympathetic. For all her venom, she is remarkably intelligent, articulate, persuasive, and—at least at the beginning of the play—a bit of the underdog because she is so thoroughly ignored and mistreated. She is, after all, manipulated, exploited, and unjustly discarded by a callous husband who simply elects to transfer his fickle affections to another younger, more valuable catch.

Early in the play Medea launches a blistering attack upon her disenchanted husband, Jason, attempting to score points and penetrate his emotional armour, while simultaneously probing to determine if he might be brought around to see things from her point of view:

> **MEDEA**
> But let that go. My questions will serve to underline your infamy. As things are now, where am I to turn? Home to my father? But when I came here with you, I betrayed my home and my country. To the wretched daughters of Pelias? They would surely give me a royal welcome to their home; I only murdered their father. For it is how it is. My loved ones at home have learned to hate me; the others, whom I need not have harmed, I have made my enemies to oblige you. And so, in return for these services you have made me envied among the women of Hellas! A wonderful, faithful husband I have in you, if I must be expelled from the country into exile, deserted by my friends, alone with my friendless children! A fine story to tell of the new bridegroom, that his children and the woman who saved his life are wandering about in aimless beggary! O Zeus, why O why have you given to mortals sure means of knowing gold from tinsel, yet men's exteriors show no mark by which to descry their rotten heart?[1]

---

1   Euripides, *Medea*, in *Ten Plays by Euripides*, trans. Moses Hadas and John McLean (New York: Bantam, 1990), 52.

Pressure in this play mounts as Medea seethes at the indignity of her situation and the injustice she feels done to her. The vitality of the play lies in the horrifying scale of her retribution. Unable to repair the deplorable situation, unable to achieve any redress, boxed in at every turn, hers is the toxic revenge of a suicide bomber.

To injure Jason in the worst way she can imagine, she eventually determines she will murder her own children, as well as the young wife-to-be. The tension that builds as the audience cringes and wonders if she will be able to suppress all her natural feelings of affection for her sons and commit the horror of infanticide is almost unbearable.

The level of her hurt and the incandescent heat of her anger define Medea, and have made her one of a handful of characters that have retained their lustre after thousands of years have passed.

OEDIPUS TYRANNUS
BY SOPHOCLES

This play, perhaps the most famous of all the Greek plays, presents as its protagonist the very epitome of the tragic figure. Each unit of action he takes only triggers another stage of his undoing. In struggling to live a moral life he uncovers immorality. In striving to overcome his fate, he fulfills the oracle. He seeks to prove his innocence, and instead proves his complicity.

The tale is thick with the ingredients of melodrama—incest, mistaken identity, murder, suicide. The element that elevates the story above this and allows one to identify with Oedipus is his relentless struggle to do the right thing. He blunders terribly. He is blind to his own failings. Still, throughout the play he plods on, striving to correct wrongs where he finds them. Indeed, if he were only to stop searching as some advise him, the implicating truths might never become known.

It is because of this—his battle to do right and his willingness to do whatever he can to repair the situation once he discovers his complicity—that the audience is permitted to view him as something more than a puppet or a pawn of fate.

Even in what appears to be a relatively simple exchange, the struggle is charged. Once again, Oedipus's stubborn insistence to make things right places him in conflict with his wife, and draws him closer to his tragic destiny.

OEDIPUS
...Is he the same fellow this man's described?

JOCASTA
It doesn't matter if he is or not.
Don't give it a thought! Just let his words go!

OEDIPUS
What! Now that we've heard all these hints and clues,
I'm to stop my birth from coming to light!

JOCASTA
Do you value your life? Drop these questions!
My suffering suffices for us both!

OEDIPUS
What are you worried for? Suppose I am
The child of slaves who were children of slaves
Born to slaves—that won't make a slave of you!

JOCASTA
Listen to me! Enough's enough! Stop, I say!

OEDIPUS
You'd prefer me to live my life a lie!

JOCASTA
My wish is for what's truly best for you.

OEDIPUS
And for years I've been oppressed by that "best"!

JOCASTA
Wretch! I hope you never learn who you are!

OEDIPUS
Won't someone go and bring that shepherd here?
Pride may well suit her noble family…!

JOCASTA
Ah, you miserable man, you! What's left
For me to say! Nothing! Nothing! Nothing![2]

Note how the conflict escalates swiftly to a point where matters are advanced. In the face of Oedipus's stubborn insistence Jocasta ultimately abandons her opposition, and the narrative presses forward.

---

2   Sophocles, *King Oedipus*, in *Sophocles, 2*, trans. Jascha Kessler (Philadelphia: University of Philadelphia Press, 1998), 78–79.

ANTIGONE
BY SOPHOCLES

If *The Eumenides* concluded that the rule of law was necessary to contain the forces of violence and chaos in society, *Antigone* takes up the argument again from the opposite end. Who will protect the rights of the individual from the relentless, impersonal machinery of the law? And for what responsibility is the individual assessed when confronted by an unjust, irresponsible law?

In this play, following the death of Antigone's two warring brothers, Eteocles and Polynices, Creon ascends to power. Because Eteocles died defending Thebes, Creon provides him with a proper hero's burial. Because Polynices played the part of traitor, attacking the walls of Thebes, Creon denies him a burial—and by extension denies his soul rest.

Faithful sister that she is, Antigone declares at the end of *Seven Against Thebes* that regardless of what parts her brothers played in the war and regardless of Creon's pronouncements, she will ensure that Polynices receives proper, funereal arrangements, as is his moral right. When an enraged Creon discovers that Polynices has received his funereal rites, he sends soldiers out to find and fetch back the criminal who has defied the law.

Antigone, brought before Creon, freely confesses to her crime, and in so doing provokes a collision between the rule of law and the moral imperatives of the individual.

CREON
Well, what do you say—you hiding your head there? Do you admit, or do you deny the deed?

ANTIGONE
I do admit it. I do not deny it.

CREON
(*to the SENTRY*) You—you may go. You are discharged from blame.

Exit SENTRY.

Now tell me, in as few words as you can,
Did you know the order forbidding such an act?

ANTIGONE
I knew it, naturally. It was plain enough.

CREON
And yet you dared to contravene it?

ANTIGONE
Yes.
That order did not come from God. Justice,
That dwells with the gods below, knows no such law.
I did not think your edicts strong enough
To overrule the unwritten unalterable laws
Of God and heaven, you being only a man.[3]

This play, with its urgent appeal to citizens everywhere to defy injustice even when confronted by all the power of a tyranny, remains vital today.

Jean Anouilh's provocative adaptation and production of the play during the German occupation of France in the Second World War offered a striking reminder of the play's true potency and eternal significance.

For playwrights surveying the Greek theatre, it is important to note that these three characters, Oedipus, Medea, and Antigone, resist the erasure of time and retain their currency with audiences today at least partially because the struggles they accept are of such magnitude that they demand tremendous effort from the protagonists, and are at the same time representative of challenges and struggles that are universal to the human condition.

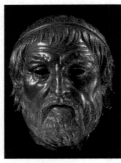

A bronze bust of Sophocles. Photograph presented with the permission of the British Museum.

---

3   Sophocles, *Antigone*, in *The Theban Plays: King Oedipus, Oedipus at Colonus, Antigone*, trans. E.F. Watling (Baltimore: The Penguin Classics, 1956), 138.

If you want to send a message, call Western Union.
> —Samuel Goldwyn

The above quotation expresses a commonly held notion of how ideas should best be treated. If there isn't exactly a fear of ideas today, there is certainly a profound sense of skepticism that the theatre is the correct forum to explore them. The theatre is considered more properly the domain of amusement and entertainment.

This wasn't the case for the Greeks, however. If the theatre was constructed to test character, it was felt important that they be tested to their core.

This may be key to understanding the ability of the Greek characters to weather time—the willingness of Greek playwrights to tackle challenging ideas and build them into the protagonist's journey. Some of these big ideas have already been mentioned. Oedipus investigates man's inescapable relationship with destiny. The *Oresteia* explores the foundation of justice. Aristophanes took on several consequential ideas: the enfranchisement of women, the notion that peace could be more beneficial than war (this at a time when the norm was that the state enriched itself by waging war), and the importance of art.

None of these propositions were small, standard, or safe. There was also the accompanying notion that a playwright should not simply be warming up old ideas, but rather should be generating something fresh and vital. Aristophanes says as much in *The Ecclesiazusae(A Parliament of Women)*:

> Love of novelty and disdain for traditions,
> These are the dominating principles among us.[4]

There has been a movement in contemporary writing to ignore the larger landscape in favour of the miniature, but it is worth considering how exhilarating it can be for an audience to confront an idea of a certain scale.

---

4   Aristophanes, *Ecclesiazusae*, trans. Anonymous, The Internet Classics Archive, http://classics.mit.edu/Aristophanes/eccles.html (accessed May 7, 2009).

6. ECONOMY ϛ′

Familiar as we are today with the great length of the Greek chorus, it's commonly assumed that the Greeks dallied and lingered over words at the expense of advancing the narrative.

While it's true that the Greeks had a different aesthetic sensibility as regards the role of the chorus in a play, it's worth considering the actual economy that the Greek playwrights employed in their storytelling.

Remember that all of the plays that we retain as examples of ancient Greek theatre are relatively short by modern standards: they are essentially the length of our contemporary one-act plays, and the point of attack that is employed is sometimes breathtakingly concise.

TROJAN WOMEN
BY EURIPIDES

The play opens upon the forlorn site of a prisoner-of-war camp. The women captured after the fall of Troy wait and wonder what their captors will choose to do with them, but Euripides doesn't force them to wait long.

Note the quick strokes applied by Euripides to render the bureaucracy that accompanies war. Watch how efficiently the herald Talthybius provides news about what has happened to Hecuba's daughters, how he attempts to prevent generating heightened emotions in the way he nonchalantly delivers the account of Polyxena's death.

TALTHYBIUS
Hecuba, you know I made many trips to Troy as a messenger from the Greek army. That makes me an acquaintance of yours, of long standing. I am Talthybius, here to announce the latest news.

HECUBA
Here it comes, my Trojan friends. This is what I have long been dreading.

TALTHYBIUS
The assignments have already been made, if that was your dread.

HECUBA
Ah! Where do we go? Some city in Thessaly or Phthia or in the land of Cadmus?

TALTHYBIUS
You were each assigned individually to separate masters.

HECUBA
Then who got whom? Is there good luck ahead for any of Troy's daughters?

TALTHYBIUS
I can tell you, but you must particularize your questions, one at a time.

HECUBA
Then tell me, who got my daughter, poor Cassandra?

TALTHYBIUS
King Agamemnon took her, as a special prize.

HECUBA
What? To be the slave of his Lacedaemonian wife? Ah me!

TALTHYBIUS
No, she is to be his concubine.

HECUBA
His concubine? The virgin of Phoebus, the girl on whom the golden-haired god bestowed virginity, as a peculiar favour?

TALYTHYBIUS
Love's shafts pierced him for the prophetic maiden.

HECUBA
O my daughter, throw away the holy branches, throw off the sacred livery of chaplets that deck your person.

TALTHYBIUS
Why? Isn't it a great thing to get a king for a lover?

HECUBA
And what of the daughter you lately took away from me? Where is she?

TALTHYBIUS
You mean Polyxena? Of whom do you speak of?

HECUBA
Just her. To whom did the lot yoke her?

TALTHYBIUS
She has been appointed to serve at the tomb of Achilles.

HECUBA
Ah me! My daughter. To serve at a tomb? But what new usage or ordinance is this that the Greeks have?

TALTHYBIUS
God bless your child. She rests well.[1]

It's fascinating to observe just how effectively rendered Talthybius is in these few short strokes. His identity and essential nature is so clearly evoked through the few specific actions and speeches he is given that he is endowed with much greater weight and presence than his actual stage time might initially suggest.

---

1   Euripides, *Trojan Women*, in *Ten Plays by Euripides*, 180.

AGAMEMNON
BY AESCHYLUS

It wasn't only in beginning stories or broaching subjects that efficiency was demonstrated. The Greek poets could be great misers with words. They believed that in writing, as in cooking, too much of even a good thing could spoil the dish. Consider how sparingly Aeschylus doles out his dialogue here, in his conclusion of the play *Agamemnon*.

Earlier, Clytemnestra (Klytaimnestra) welcomed her husband, King Agamemnon, home from the wars with Troy. To celebrate his triumph, she invited him to enter the palace along a red carpet she has specially spread for the occasion, and she has had him draped in his robes of office. Once inside the palace, however, the weighty robes act as a straight-jacket, and Clytemnestra swiftly revenges herself on her husband for his earlier sacrifice of their daughter, Iphigenia. She withdraws a knife and butchers him along with the concubine he has fetched back from the battle, Cassandra. Then, with the king out of the way, Clytemnestra seizes power along with her lover, Aigisthos.

A crowd of distressed citizens form at the palace gates, but without a leader to organize the mob and incite action, they are unable to formulate a plan.

Pay special attention to the swift manner in which Aeschylus closes this play, the understatement he employs in the haunting final declaration.

KLYTAIMNESTRA
Old men, elders of Argos, go home.
Go home, before you regret what will come.
What's done is done.
Accept.
Pray that the evil that gorges on Argive death
Has had his fill. He has held us in his talons
Far too long.

AIGISTHOS
But you can't!
Listen to them!
Their foul mouths spitting out
Flowers of evil! Testing their luck—
How far they can go!

I'm in charge here!
The new leader!
Master!

OLD MAN
No real Argive grovels to murderers.

AIGISTHOS
Then real Argives will have to be taught.

OLD MAN
Not if Orestes comes home first.

AIGISTHOS
Exiles feed on hope. I know.

OLD MAN
Grow fat, while you can! Pollute justice!

AIGISTHOS
Fool! You'll pay for this one day!

OLD MAN
Cock of the walk! Strut for your hen!

KLYTAIMNESTRA
Ignore them. They're nothing.
Idle barkers.
We rule here now.
We have the power.
Together you and I will set all things
Right.[2]

Clytemnestra takes the hand of Aigisthos and together they enter the palace, the doors shutting behind them.

The citizens, remembering the tortured cries of Agamemnon and Cassandra, continue to linger in the streets and protest. There's some ineffectual name-calling, but Clytemnestra, having dismissed the rabble,

---

2   Aeschylus, *Agamemnon*, in *Aeschylus: The Complete Plays, Vol. 1*, trans. Carl R. Mueller (Hanover: A Smith and Kraus Books, 2002), 152.

reassures her lover that in the end what matters is that they hold the reigns of office.

"We have the power. Together you and I will set all things right," the queen murmurs—and then draws the curtain on the play. Not one word extra. In that brevity everything that has to be said is said, and it is utterly chilling.

The gates to the ruins of Mycenae, the fortress associated with Agamemnon and the House of Atreus.

7. CONTRAST ζ′

If you wish to create an economical theatre, and feature only a few independent characters on stage—and yet at the same time hope to offer a sense of the breadth and scope of an entire world—it is essential that you martial your resources and develop a strategy. The Greeks had developed such a strategy, and it can be encapsulated in a single word: contrast.

Contrast allows a writer to generate a palette upon which the colours and tones of the world may be mixed. It establishes the poles and parameters of that world, and it permits the construction of a narrative that offers a thesis and antithesis from which to develop a genuine dialectic.

HECUBA
BY EURIPIDES

Euripides's play *Hecuba* presents the struggle of Hecuba (Hekabe) following the fall of Troy. Hecuba attempts to salvage what she can from the ruins of her kingdom, but portion by portion she sees those things that are dear to her taken and destroyed. She soon discovers that her daughter Polyxena has been selected for sacrifice at the tomb of Achilles, as a tribute to the fallen hero.

Early in *Hecuba* two central figures are established in striking contrast to one another—the mother, Hecuba, active, resistant, resentful, driven; and the daughter, Polyxena, calm, accepting, and stoic.[1]

Between these two extremities, Euripides is able to investigate a recurrent theme regarding the manner in which destiny can be met.

HEKABE
O daughter, my words for your murder go into the air,
  pointless.
But you, if you have any power more than a mother has,
Now is the time—let loose your nightingale's wail—
So your life be not torn from you!
Fall at Odysseus' knee,
Persuade him. You have a claim!
Yes he has children himself—he may pity your luck!

POLYXENA
I see you, Odysseus,
How you hide your right hand in your cloak,
How you turn your face away.
Afraid I'll supplicate?
Don't worry.
You're safe.
I will go with you.
Because it is necessary.
And because I want to die.
Unwilling—I'd look like a coward.

---

1   Anne Carson, *Grief Lessons: Four Plays by Euripides* (New York: NYRB Classics, 2008), 115.

Like a woman in love with her life.
But why live?[2]

In their approaches to overwhelming opposition, in their approaches to death, in their approaches to their respective *fates*, they could not be more different. This literary device provides not only a more dynamic portrait of the mother and daughter, but by extension a more dynamic portrait of their world.

---

2   Euripides, *Hekabe*, in *Grief Lessons: Four Plays by Euripides*, trans. Anne Carson (New York: NYRB Classics, 2008), 115.

ANTIGONE
BY SOPHOCLES

When crafting characters who have sprung from the same family, writers are continually presented with a similar problem. How does one present characters that both closely resemble one another and so indicate the bonds of blood and nurture, and at the same time offer characters who stand apart from one another in temperament and disposition.

This too requires a display of contrast, and in the play *Antigone*, Sophocles succeeds rather strikingly in doing just this with the sisters Antigone and Ismene.

Antigone, outraged by Creon's sanction of her brother, determines to provide Polynices a burial regardless of the law. She approaches her sister to seek support, but receives a cautious warning instead.

> **ISMENE**
> Sister, remember what happened to our father!
> How he was shunned, disgraced, and, overcome
> with self-loathing, condemned himself to blindness.
> Remember Mother. When she learned she was also
> his mother, she hanged herself. And don't forget
> our brothers killed each other. Think about
> the fact that we're all that's left of our family.
> If we went against Creon, would we not die
> The worst deaths yet?
>
> We're just women, you know,
> not powerful enough to go up against men.
> Have you forgotten that the strong control
> the weak? We have to obey Creon's orders,
> this one and any others. I will ask the dead
> to forgive me for obeying the law. It would be
> a grave mistake to do anything else.
>
> **ANTIGONE**
> Forget it, Is. If that is how you feel,
> I wouldn't let you come if you begged to.
> You can go do whatever you want to do;
> I'll bury him by myself. So what if I die!

It's for a good cause. I'll lie next to him
and make him happy forever, for that's how long
Death lasts.
You do what you want, since it's obvious
that you don't care about doing what's right.[3]

In the choices they take, Sophocles swiftly paints a compelling picture of two siblings who embody completely and utterly different pre-
dispositions: Antigone, passionate, action-oriented, bold, assured; and
Ismene, conservative, reflective, anxious, and uncertain.

The craft used to evoke these two is such that one cannot listen to
the one character without thinking upon the difference of the other, so
not only are the two set apart, but each in turn serves to illuminate some
opposing aspect of the other.

---

3   Sophocles, *Antigone*, in *Sophocles, 2*, trans. Kelly Cherry (Philadelphia:
University of Philadelphia Press, 1998), 195–196.

THE CLOUDS
BY ARISTOPHANES

Of course, the applications of contrast for comic effect were not lost on the Greeks. Consider how Aristophanes contrasts these two characters, Strepsiades, and Student 1, in the *Clouds*.

Strepsiades is a simple country fellow who has heard that the Socratic school will provide him with sufficient learning to argue his way out of the debts he owes. He knocks at the entrance to the school and as the door opens is immediately upbraided by one of the students for causing a disturbance.

STUDENT 1
You're a fool whoever you are,
Banging and clattering at the door
Without thinking; but I was thinking
And you've given me a miscarriage.

STREPSIADES
I'm so sorry. I come from the country.
What have I made miscarry? Tell me.

STUDENT 1
Oh, I couldn't. It wouldn't be right
Except to a fellow student—see what I mean?

STREPSIADES
You can tell me. You see I've come
To enroll at this Logic Factory.

STUDENT 1
All right, I'll tell you, but you've got
To remember these things are sacred mysteries.
(in awed tones) Socrates asked Chairephon
A few minutes ago how many lengths
Of its own foot could a flea jump.
(After biting Chairephon it hopped
out of his eyebrow on to the smooth
Curve of the Master's head.)

STREPISADES
And how did Chairephon cope
With this weighty problem?

STUDENT 1
(seriously) Ever
So cleverly! He warmed some wax,
Then grabbed the flea and plunged its feet
Into the wax and, you see, when the wax
Cooled off the flea had on a pair
Of Persian slippers which Chairephon then
Took off and used them to measure
The space between.

STREPSIADES
Almighty Zeus,
What amazing subtlety of mind![4]

The use of contrast has become such a common feature of theatrical writing that writers pursuing the craft today sometimes take it for granted. We find it employed to good effect in plays as varying in tone and style as Shakespeare's *Comedy of Errors*, Sam Shepard's *Farther West*, Pinter's *Dumb Waiter* and Neil Simon's *Odd Couple*, but it is important for writers to recollect how long this strategy has been utilized and why it has been so widely deployed.

---

4   Aristophanes, *The Clouds*, in *Aristophanes: Plays One*, trans. Patric Dickinson (Oxford: Oxford University Press, 1970), 114.

8. AUTHORITY η′

One of the standard axioms of contemporary creative writing pedagogy is to "write what you know." It's intriguing to see a methodology of a personalized connection to narrative slowly developing in Greek literature, as drama became a fully realized art form.

As the concept of creative writing was developing, so was a parallel notion of creative "process." Of course, no how-to books existed at the time (some have come to understand Aristotle's *Poetics* as a kind of "how-to" book, but as discussed earlier in this text, this was firstly only Aristotle's best *analysis* of literature, and secondly only the rough notes for his oral lectures), but one can get a fairly accurate idea of how writers worked by examining the body of work they left behind.

There is, as mentioned earlier, a sense that the Greek playwrights were initially working from a template provided by tradition, mythology, and ritual. Yet as the Greek theatre developed, expectations surrounding the craft changed, and the process itself began to alter. A number of the works of the Greeks can be viewed as very personal statements.

Aeschylus was, as mentioned prior, both a writer and a solider. In his capacity as an Athenian soldier, he participated in at least one of the most historically significant battles—the Battle of Marathon.

His play *The Persians* reflects something of that personal experience. We know from references in ancient documents that he and his brother Cynaegirus fought at Marathon against the Persians. This matchup between Persians and Greeks was of such an unequal nature that it was hard to conceive that the Greeks could possibly win. But through the application of superior tactics, the Greeks left the battlefield victorious.

This conflict was repeated again when Xerxes, the son of Darius, ascended to the Persian throne. Again, the forces that met in combat seemed so overwhelmingly mismatched that there appeared to be no way that the Greeks could win. The peril that Greeks faced, and their surprising deliverance at Salamis had a powerful impact upon the Greek psyche.

THE PERSIANS
BY AESCHYLUS

There is no certainty that Aeschylus fought at Salamis. If he did he didn't bother to ensure that it was noted in his memorial inscription upon his tombstone. ("This tomb the dust of Aeschylus doth hide, Euphorian's son and fruitful Gela's pride. How tried his valor, Marathon may tell, and long haired Medes who knew it too well.")

However, the description in *The Persians* of the struggle in the waters beyond Salamis is so detailed and offers such an overarching vision of the events from beginning to end that historians have since leaned upon it for an understanding of how naval battles of the time were waged. It indicates either a thorough knowledge of this particular battle, or at the very least a thorough knowledge of this *kind* of battle.

> **HERALD**
> From our side then, cries, shouts in answer.
> There was no delaying now.
> Ship struck ship, ramming with bows of brass, breaking
>   away whole prows.
> The Greeks began it. Men on opposing decks let fly their
>   spears.
> We resisted at first, holding our own; but soon our ships,
>   so massed together, struck each other head-on in the
>   narrow strait, bronze beak ramming bronze beak,
>   destroying oars and benches.
> The Greeks then circled round in perfect order and struck,
>   and hulls were tumbled wrong-side up, and the sea was
>   no longer seen for all the wreckage and floating bodies.
> And all the shores and reefs bobbing with corpses.[1]

There can be no doubt that it was at least partially his experience as a soldier that informed the writing of Aeschylus, and provided this play with the authenticity that arises out of practical knowledge. As well, the emotional core of the play is so powerfully expressed that one feels that it could only come from the deeply felt emotions resulting from having been in such a struggle.

---

1   Aeschylus, *The Persians*, in *Aeschylus: The Complete Plays*, Vol. 2, 142.

THE ACHARNIANS
BY ARISTOPHANES

In another vein, but equally demonstrating a very individual process, was the work of Aristophanes. His comedic works were unashamedly personal in tone and in character. The majority of his writing reflects his experiences and his perspective on the events of his times. He adamantly opposed the war between Athens and Sparta and his plays were rich with material that both reflected these views, and lobbied on their behalf.

Consider the opening comments that Dicaeopolis offers at the commencement of *The Acharnians*. As the play opens, Athens is at war with Sparta, and has been for some time. Dicaeopolis has arrived at the Athenian assembly to lobby on behalf of a peaceful resolution to the war. As he waits for citizens to arrive, he glances around at his surroundings and makes these astute observations:

> ...A day fixed for the Assembly and come the dawn, not a soul on the Pnyx. They're all nattering away in the market square and dodging the whips. Not even the principals are here. They'll arrive late, of course, elbowing one another, charging en masse, making a beeline for the front row—you've no idea. As for being concerned with peace, they don't give a damn... O City, my poor City!"[2]

Even in these short, trenchant musings one understands that the writer of this passage is an individual who possesses first-hand knowledge of these events. It is evident in every dot and detail of his observations.

2   Aristophanes, *The Acharnians*, in *Aristophanes: The Complete Plays*, trans. Paul Roche (New York: New American Library, 2005), 7.

THE FROGS
BY ARISTOPHANES

As a writer, Aristophanes was also clearly interested in, and familiar with, matters pertaining to writing. Though *The Frogs* is offered through the filter of myth, there is plainly a portion of the text devoted to examination of the craft of writing in terms of style, voice, and appropriate content. Listen to Heracles and Dionysus discussing the present abominable state of writing.

HERACLES
But don't we have a whole horde of babies today,
    churning out tragedies
and outbabbling Euripides by the mile?

DIONYSUS
They're nonentities, all,
Like swallows twittering away
And murdering their art. And though they have the gall
To wangle themselves a chorus,
After they've pissed all over Tragedy, they're never heard
    of again.
Meanwhile, you can hunt for a poet of consequence,
Someone capable of a memorable line,
And you won't find a single one.[3]

It can be assumed that Aristophanes intended this as a critique of the literature of his times and those who wrote it, as well as an analysis of writing in general, but he was an accomplished enough playwright to find a way to render this essentially intellectual quest in a more physical and visual manner. To perform this analysis, he sends his protagonist on a mission to Hades to retrieve a "real" poet.

Once in Hades, Aristophanes uses the opportunity to accuse Euripides, who languishes there with Aeschylus, of diminishing the power of writing.

---

3   Aristophanes, *The Frogs*, in *Aristophanes: The Complete Plays*, trans. Paul Roche (New York: New American Library, 2005), 544–545.

AESCHYLUS
You put decent women married to decent men
In a situation like that of Bellerophon
That drives them to suicide.

EURIPIDES
All right, but I didn't invent the plot of Phaedra.

AESCHYLUS
Worse luck, no! But the poet shouldn't side with what is
    evil and display it on stage like a demonstration.
Children may have teachers but adults have the poet and
    the poet ought to keep things on a higher plane.

EURIPIDES
(*sarcastically*) As high as Mount Lycabettus, no doubt,
    or lofty Parnassus, and they're to be our instructors in
    the good?

AESCHYLUS
Listen, you miserable heel, the lofty thought and the high
    ideal call for a language to match.[4]

In this brief passage, Aristophanes has inspected the meaning of writing and the manner in which it should be executed. In these passages and others one begins to see the personal and the particular voice transforming writing, establishing authority and specificity.

---

4   Ibid., 587.

9. TRANSFORMATION θ′

Theatre has come to be associated with change—in fact, theatre can be viewed as a kind of chronicle of change. It carefully records the exchange of one status quo for another and offers a demonstration of how these changes are made possible. How do men become possessed by a desire for power, willing to take whatever action to attain the highest post or position? *Macbeth* presents some telling analysis. How can an obsession for money lead a man to become alienated from family, friends, and society? Molière's *Miser* details that particular journey.

In the Greek theatre the transformation of the individual began to take on some importance, and could be manifested in a variety of ways. The transformation might be one involving hierarchical stature—the dominant authority and sovereign power brought low. Oedipus obsessively pursues the truth and is consequently transformed from the most exalted, most respected, potent figure in his kingdom to someone disgraced, cursed, exiled, blinded, and beggared.

Medea is alchemized and elevated from the bitter, rejected spouse observed at the beginning of the play of the same name, into an avenging, triumphant, god-like figure.

Even the beloved demigod, Heracles, might be transfigured.

HERACLES
BY EURIPIDES

Heracles (Herakles) returns home from his troubled labours, ridding the world of monsters, returning from hell—literally—where he has gone to fetch the three-headed dog Cerberus, and discovers that his family has been marginalized, terrorized, and are about to be executed by the local tyrant. He first slays the tyrant, then, in what some have seen as an almost clinical description of post-traumatic stress disorder, is "transformed" and in a blind killing frenzy, murders his wife and children.

This surprising, and surprisingly disturbing transformation, is described best by the chorus.

> The sons are his prey
> His eyes are ablaze
> He is full of the god, like a forest in flames
> The revel begins.
> The children haven't got a chance.[1]

When he awakens from the frenzy, the metamorphosis has been so sudden, so unexpected, so complete that he remembers virtually nothing of it. In a moment he has been transformed from a beloved hero and cultural icon into an unbalanced mass murderer.

---

1   Euripides, *Herakles*, in *Herakles Gone Mad: Rethinking Heroism in an Age of Endless War*, trans. Robert Emmet Meagher (Northampton, MA: Olive Branch Press, 2006), 105.

THE BIRDS
BY ARISTOPHANES

The Birds presents a stunningly physical transformation. In this play two Athenian men, burdened with debt and utterly disenchanted with society, attempt to join the birds in their world. Though first rejected by the birds (who scorn humans) the two men, Euelpides and Peisetairus, at last grow wings, join forces with and ultimately co-create a heavenly land with the birds: Cloudcuckooland. Eventually, Peisetairus is transformed even further into something approaching a deity, as he is delivered the lightning bolts of Zeus and the hand of the princess in marriage.

The final stages of the transformation are described by the chorus:

> Behold, he comes
> More radiant than a shooting star
> Flashing its diamond path along—
> Yea, even the flames
> Of the lancing sun's scintillating rays...
> So your master comes, conducting here
> A bride beautiful beyond compare
> And wielding the winged thunderbolt of Zeus.
> A perfume without name
> Floats up through the fathoms of the air, profuse,
> And breezes waft the weaving smoke of incense
> In a wondrous way. [2]

Peisetairus enters leading the princess with one hand and clutching a cluster of thunderbolts with the other, his exchange of status complete.

---

[2] Aristophanes, *The Birds*, in *Aristophanes: The Complete Plays*, trans. Paul Roche (New York: New American Library, 2005), 412.

THE BACCHAE
BY EURIPIDES

The Bacchae is not only a play rich in transformation, it is a play that in one sense dissects and examines the very meaning of transformation.

As the play opens, the immortal Dionysus appears and addresses the audience, informing us that he has gained converts wherever he has journeyed in Asia, and now he visits Thebes to convince those that doubt that his cult is genuinely inspired and led by a god.

Chief among skeptics is Pentheus, King of Thebes. He first imprisons Dionysus, mistaking him, walking the earth in human form as he is, for an acolyte of the new religion.

When the god is freed by mysterious forces, Pentheus threatens to imprison him once again. Instead, Dionysus offers to guide Pentheus to spy upon the secret rites. Pentheus accepts the invitation, and aware that he must be in disguise, wraps himself in women's robes. Once the disguise is in place, however, a more dramatic transformation begins almost at once.

> *THE STRANGER calls upon PENTHEUS to come out.*

THE STRANGER
Pentheus! If you are so eager to pry into secret things, so bent on evil, come out in front of the house; let us see how you look dressed like a woman, a Bacchic maenad, off to spy on your mother and her company.

> *Enter PENTHEUS in Bacchic attire; he moves and speaks as if under some strange influence.*

You do look like one of Cadmus's daughters.

PENTHEUS
I seem to see two suns, and a double Thebes, ay, two seven-gated cities. And a bull is leading me on—you seem to be a bull, with horns growing on your head. Were you ever an animal? Certainly you have the look of a bull.

THE STRANGER
The god is our escort. He was hostile before, but now he has made peace with us. Now you see as you should.

PENTHEUS
What do I look like? Have I not the pose of Ino? Or Agave, yes, my own mother Agave?[3]

It is clear that once dressed in his disguise, Pentheus has become possessed and completely transformed. In this altered state he is led by the god Dionysus to view the sacred Bacchic rites. Once there, he is betrayed by the god, spied by the Maenads, chased, captured, and torn to pieces.

The change that Pentheus undergoes is physical, visual, and ultimately highly theatrical. But one can also understand the transformation as an external and metaphorical rendering of the internal and hidden desires of this character—a process that only lends itself to the essential impulse of the theatre, which is to illuminate the hidden, and by so doing penetrate the true nature of character.

---

3   Euripides, *The Bacchants*, in *Ten Plays by Euripides*, trans. Moses Hadas and John McLean (New York: Bantam, 1990), 301.

10. THE INFLUENCE OF ARISTOTLE ı′

The great paintings, sculptures and architectural projects of the Renaissance seem to resemble those of ancient Greece and Rome, rather than those of the Middle Ages; this was deliberate. There was, from the mid-fourteenth century onwards, an increasing search for the manuscripts of classical authors, and their writings and opinions became the subject of detailed analyses and wholesale emulation by scholars, who called themselves "humanists." Some studied the writings of Aristotle, and went on to write philosophy, like Marsilio Ficino (1433–99) or Giovanni Pico della Mirandola (1463–94).

—Geoffrey Parker, *The World*

The *Poetics* seems, on the face of it, an unlikely work to have achieved so seminal a status. Incomplete, substantially afflicted by textual corruptions; somewhat disproportionate in its treatment both of types and of aspects of Greek poetry, rarely as full as we might like it to be in its elucidation of its leading ideas...

—Stephen Halliwell,
"*The Poetics* and Its Interpreters"

It is a testament to groundbreaking work that was occurring in Greece in these very early days that the figures who are most revered and remembered today are the thinkers, planners, and innovators of the time.

Aristotle conquered no cities, constructed no temples, and was actually a teacher more than anything else, but his observations influenced not only Western civilization and thought, but through Islamic culture, Eastern civilization and thought as well.

It is arguably his writings in *Poetics* that most shaped the arts, but he had a very agile mind and he covered a lot of ground. His detailed notes described thoughts on such wide-ranging topics as physics, metaphysics, nature, and ethics and influenced so many things that it is difficult to overestimate his importance.

After Rome conquered the Greeks, the Greeks had their revenge. Their thoughts, perceptions, and methods were so widely adopted that it was difficult to tell who had conquered whom. Aristotle's writings were especially prized and it was during the Roman era that his notes were edited and fully catalogued. After Rome fell, communication throughout the former empire collapsed and his writings disappeared only to reappear later in the ninth century when Arab scholars translated his works and introduced them to the Islamic world.

When the European and Arabic worlds collided again as a result of the regrettable Crusades, one side benefit was that Aristotle's observations were reintroduced to Europe where they had considerable impact. St. Thomas Aquinas studied Aristotle and wrote his famous *Summa Theologica* in which he reconciled Aristotle's beliefs and Christianity. Aristotle's works were widely disseminated and became the foundation for a new way of thinking. European universities coalesced around a core of "Aristotelian" concepts, including the application of logic, a philosophy of nature, metaphysics, and morality, and of course a new understanding of literature. This revisioning of knowledge in turn helped to propel the dawning of a new age: the Renaissance.

What clarity can Aristotle be said to have brought to the dramatic form? He first and foremost performed analysis, and then as a consequence of his investigations he produced a series of clear, concise definitions.

1. He proposed that a play was an "imitation of an action."

"Tragedy is an imitation of an action that is admirable, complete and possesses magnitude..."[1]

This statement, as simple as it is, is far from obvious. People, in their discussions of the theatre, often become confused about the function of a play. Characters talk in plays, and so they believe that plays are *about* dialogue. There are memorable individuals in plays, and so people believe plays *describe* those individuals. But the former can better be captured in a recorded conversation, and the latter is better captured in a biography.

In fact, plays are about many things, including character and dialogue, but the characters appearing in plays are first and foremost defined

---

1   Aristotle, *Poetics*, 10.

by action, decisions, and choices. In short, individuals are best defined by what they *do*, and what they are *seen to do*.

2. He posited the primacy of plot.

> Tragedy is not an imitation of persons, but of actions and of life. Well-being and ill being reside in action, and the goal of life is an activity, not a quality; people possess certain qualities in accordance with their character, but they achieve well-being or its opposite on the basis of how they fare. So the imitation of character is not the purpose of what the agents do; character is included along with and on account of the actions. *So the events, i.e., the plot, are what tragedy is there for, and that is the most important thing of all.*[2] (Italics are mine)

The Greeks were fond of offering written descriptions of characters, supplemented with anecdotes and bits and pieces of dialogue. Aristotle recognized that the essential feature that separated this biographical material from a play was the mechanism of plot, which served to demonstrate character within a prescribed narrative arc, rather than generally describe character.

It is important to note, however, there was nothing in his writing to suggest that he wished to diminish the importance of character, but rather he implied that the best way to achieve character was through the application of plot.

3. He maintained that unity was a critical quality of a good plot.

It is the mark of an important thought that once it occurs, it appears so obvious that it feels impossible that it could ever have been overlooked. This is certainly the case when one thinks of Aristotle's writings on unity.

That a play should be framed around a single defining element seems perfectly clear to writers today—but this concept, perhaps more than any other, has been distorted and misinterpreted over the centuries, and has been the subject of tremendous controversy.

From the sixteenth century to the mid-eighteen hundreds, because of a misinterpretation of Aristotle's thoughts as described in the *Poetics*, it was felt that a well-made play must occur within a twenty-four hour

---

2   Ibid., 4:3.

period and that it must occur in one geographic location. The unadorned elegance of Aristotle's definition of unity is, however, summed up in one simple statement "…the structure of the various sections of the events must be such that the transposition or removal of any one section dislocates and changes the whole."[3]

It is clear that the unity that he is speaking of has more to do with the embracing and organizing unity of the overarching action of the play than of some kind of technical formula involving numbers of days or locations.

4. He argued that consequence was critical to the integrity of a narrative.

"There is an important difference between a set of events happening because of certain other events and after certain other events."[4]

In this statement one can see Aristotle applying some of his analysis to the granular aspects of narrative. He implied that the critical elements of story and, by extension, plot, the things that separated it from a mere chronicle of related events, were the twin notions of cause and effect.

For writers, this is an immensely helpful concept to retain because it provides a connecting bridge between the inner desires of the character and the flow of action that is plot.

5. And he enjoined that the action be visual.

"When constructing plots and working them out complete with their linguistic expression, one should so far as possible visualize what is happening."[5]

Although Aristotle focused primarily on the literary aspect of theatrical writing—the poetics—it is apparent in this injunction that he understood and acknowledged something of the distinctly performative and visual nature of a play. This acknowledgement that there was something in the way that the play was viewed that separated it from other forms of writing, while not elaborated upon in his notes, was of sufficient importance that he ensured that it was included in his lectures.

Aristotle's writings contained flaws. There are certain passages in the *Poetics*, for instance, that are not entirely clear. Heated discussion continues to this day regarding what precisely is meant by his remarks relating to the "purging of emotion." Unfortunately, there are places where Aristotle's writing is incomplete. The commentary devoted to analysis of comedy, for instance, is so thin as to be almost

---

3   Ibid., 5:4.
4   Ibid., 6:2.
5   Ibid., 8:3.

insignificant. There are some statements that just don't withstand scrutiny. (There is a strain of misogyny that runs through his writing, for instance, that is not uncommon among the ancient Greeks.) But each of these five elements is of enormous use to any writer.

The Gutenberg Bible has been said to have transformed Europe, not because the Bible had not already existed—of course it had, in the form of the hundreds of laboriously handwritten manuscripts that abbeys and monks had produced—but because the ability to mass produce the Bible through use of the printing press provided many thousands more people with access to it. In a curious fashion, Aristotle did something similar.

The structure of drama had already existed, but as a result of Aristotle's notes, a greater number of people were provided with a common language for the analysis and discussion of the theatrical form. As a consequence of his thoughts, efforts, and writing, those interested in discussing plays were equipped with a specific set of tools that they could employ.

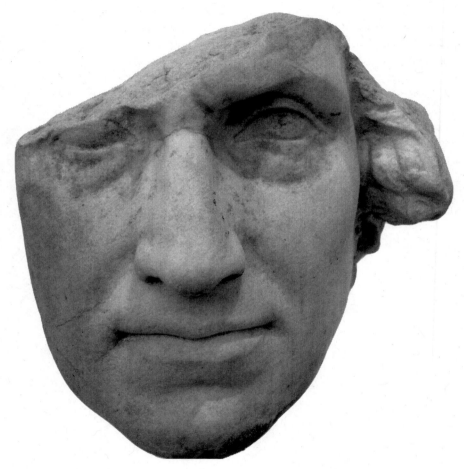

Portrait of unidentified poet. Photograph presented with the permission of the National Archeological Museum of Athens.

FINAL THOUGHTS

11. CONCLUSIONS ια′

In the end, what do the ancient Greeks have to say to contemporary playwriting?

On one level, it's not so much what the playwrights have to say as it is the manner that playwriting matured and germinated during their tenure that may be important. Contemporary playwrights can afford to closely consider the past development of the Greek plays and what it truly represents. The story of the evolution of the theatre is the story of a society striving to better understand its citizens. That is not an unworthy goal for art.

It may also be useful, however, to review the works of the ancient Greeks to discover what elements have been most successful and retained currency. As writers interested in writing, it can only be of benefit to investigate why certain works have survived and thrived. In addition, there are particular skills demonstrated in the works of Aeschylus, Euripides, Sophocles, and Aristophanes that deserve additional study and reflection. There remain treasures to be uncovered in these texts.

Finally, it may prove profitable to consider the vitality of the Greek theatre and contrast it with the struggling, haunted status of contemporary theatre. The Greeks considered theatre consequential and attendance was a part of common practice for the average citizen. Today there is a feeling that theatre has been increasingly marginalized, and even in our most cosmopolitan cities it is attended by only a very small fraction of the population.

In the world of literature, as in the world of theatre, it has become nearly standard practice to extol the benefits of a non-linear plot, a deconstructed plot, a plot unencumbered by the limitations of tradition, a plot that is simultaneously more sophisticated and more self-aware and at the same time so formless it is nearly vapour. Plot has somehow come to be perceived as the literary equivalent of a corset. Slightly out of date, extraordinarily difficult to wrestle into place, and highly constricting.

One can understand these feelings of disenchantment. They result in part from the avalanche we find ourselves under. There are simply so many more sources generating story than ever before in our history. We are literally bombarded by stories created for film, television, and the requirements of the Internet. In the haste to fill this galaxy of screens, an industrialized conveyor-belt sensibility can seem to be applied to the creative process. Stories simply appear to be recycled or cannibalized. It's only natural that audiences—and creators—should feel boredom and resentment.

And yet I recently attended a meeting of writers where one confessed—and I use the word "confessed" in the sense that the speaker was embarrassed and humbled by her revelation—that she actually enjoyed the readability of text. Although she wanted to, and expected to, appreciate the text for its sophisticated use of language and its penetrating analysis, she found herself instead charmed by the cheaper, baser elements of plot. Others present at the time listening, silently nodded their agreement. As though participating in some kind of literary twelve-step program, they too acknowledged the guilty pleasures of plot.

People yearn for story. We are born with a desire deeply imbedded within us, and there is no denying the inescapable feelings of pleasure, satisfaction, and fulfillment that come from encountering plot.

Sports—theatre's distant relative from ancient times—continues to thrive as it offers its own brand of storytelling. It has positioned itself as a populist form, providing content for millions of eager spectators each year. It is, in short, a very successful brand of contemporary theatre. And one can understand its popularity. It is perhaps the most accessible of the visual narrative forms. Viewing a sporting event doesn't require any rigorous prior study. It is possible for people from a variety of cultures, who may speak different languages, to sit in the same arena and thoroughly enjoy their collective experience. The story they receive is simple, but it is deliverable to a diverse audience, and in each instance it arrives at a definite, highly emotional conclusion and resolution. The spectators transcend their differences in those final moments and instead are bound by their shared observations. And as they depart the stadium they still pose the same questions. What constitutes strength of character? How should one behave under conditions of adversity? Is it possible, through sacrifice and supreme effort, to achieve one's goals?

But the lessons provided by sporting endeavours remain as limited in scope now as they did over two thousand years ago, and to better understand the more complicated social and emotional challenges that we encounter in our lives, we still require different tests and ultimately will arrive at different truths.

Story and its struggles provide those tests and guide us to those truths. And the theatre with its real-time, intimate, face-to-face encounters with other human beings is ideally positioned to administer those tests. Frustrated as we may be, we do not serve writing by fleeing story. Instead, we have to strip away what is false, search for what is true, and begin again.

THE END

APPENDIX — TIMELINE

To offer a clearer picture of how coinciding events related one to the other, this short timeline of events is included.

Given the scarcity of conclusive evidence, many of these dates should only be viewed as approximates.

1600–1100   Duration of the Mycenaean Civilization.

1100–800   Mycenaen culture collapses. Beginning of the Dark Ages in Greece.

800 (?) - 750   The Greek alphabet, based upon the Phoenician alphabet, is introduced. This alphabet proves popular and is soon widely employed.

Eighth Century BCE

776   The first Olympic Games are organized and subsequently held every four years. The games, founded to honour the gods, are initially comprised of one event—a foot race extending the length of the stadium.

750–700   Homer's poems—or possibly the poems of several poets operating from an oral tradition that assigns the poems to Homer—are recorded in writing.

720   The Olympics acquire a second event when another foot race is added, this one demanding sprinters run two times the length of the stadium.

704   The Olympic Games expand once again, this time to include wrestling and the pentathlon.

Seventh Century BCE

684	Boxing is added to the Olympics.
680	Chariot racing is introduced to the Olympics.
648	A combative sport blending wrestling and boxing, and called the pankration is added to the Olympics.
632	Athens abolishes the monarchy and is instead governed by an oligarchy. The popularity of the Olympic Games grows, as it becomes a five-day event.
625	The dithyrambic choruses are produced by Arion at Corinth.
621	Draco implements a severe (Draconian) code of law upon Athens.

Sixth Century BCE

594	Solon is given authority to reform the Draconian laws. These reforms provide the foundation for Athenian democracy.
582	The continued growth of institutionalized athletic events. The Pythian Games are established at Delphi and the Isthmian Games at Corinth.
546	Following a struggle for power, Pisistratus becomes tyrant of Athens.
540–527	Pisistratus modifies the Greater Dionysia and introduces Drama.
536–527	Thespis produces tragedy at the festival of the Greater Dionysia in Athens.

525   Aeschylus is born.

520   A new event is introduced to the Olympics, the hopli-
                    todromos. This is a race in which the participants wear
                    armour.

508   Reform of the Athenian code of law by Cleisthenes. He
                    establishes a democratic constitution.

500   The satyr play is introduced to Athens by Pratinus of
                    Phlius.

Fifth Century BCE

499–496   The work of Aeschylus is featured for the first time in
                    dramatic competition.

497   Athens supports an uprising against Persian influence.
                    The Persian Wars commence.

496   Sophocles is born.

493   The Theatre of Dionysus is constructed.

490   Greeks defeat Darius and the Persian army at the Battle
                    of Marathon.

485   Euripides is born.

484   Aeschylus wins in dramatic competition.
                    Herodotus, the "Father of History," is born.

480   The Persian army advances into Greece under the leader-
                    ship of Xerxes. The Greeks outmanoeuver the Persians
                    and defeat them in a naval battle at Salamis.

479   The Greeks impose a decisive defeat upon the Persian
                    army at the Battle of Plataea.

472   Aeschylus's *Persians* is produced.

470   Socrates is born.

467   Aeschylus's *Seven Against Thebes* is produced.

463   Aeschylus's *Suppliants* is produced.

460   Hippocrates is born. Thucydides is born.

458   Aeschylus's *Oresteia* (*Agamemnon*, *The Libation Bearers*, and *The Eumenides*) is produced.

456   The death of Aeschylus.

450   Aristophanes is born.

450–430   Sophocles's *Ajax* and *Trachinian Women* are produced.

449   Herodotus writes *The Histories*, a chronicle of the Persian Wars.

442   Sophocles's *Antigone* is produced.

438   Euripides's *Alestis* is produced.

431   The Peloponnesian War breaks out. Sparta attacks Athens. Euripides's *Medea* is produced.

430–428   Euripides's *Heracleidae* is produced.

429–425   Sophocles's *Oedipus Tyrannus* is produced.

428   Euripides's *Hippolytus* is produced.

427   Plato is born.

425   Aristophanes's *Acharnians* is produced.
             Euripides's *Andromache* is produced.
             Death of Herodotus.

424	Aristophanes's *Knights* is produced.
	Euripides's *Hecuba* is produced.
423	Aristophanes's *Clouds* is produced.
	Euripides's *Suppliant Maidens* is produced.
422	Aristophanes's *Wasps* is produced.
421	Aristophanes's *Peace* is produced.
420–410	Sophocles's *Electra* is produced.
417–415	Euripides's *Electra* and *Heracles* are produced.
415	Euripides's *Trojan Women* is produced
414	Aristophanes's *Birds* is produced.
	Euripides's *Ion* is produced.
413	Euripides's *Iphigeneia in Tauris* is produced.
412	Euripides's *Helen* is produced.
411	Aristophanes's *Lysistrata* is produced.
	Aristophanes's *Women Celebrating at Thesmophoria* is produced.
410	Euripides's *Phoenician Women* is produced.
409	Sophocles's *Philoctetes* is produced.
408	Euripides's *Orestes* is produced.
406	The death of Euripides.
	The death of Sophocles.
405	Euripides's *Bacchae* and *Iphigeneia at Aulis* are produced posthumously.
	Aristophanes's *Frogs* is produced.

404	End of Peloponnesian War, Athens is defeated.
401	Sophocles's *Oedipus at Colonus* is produced. Thucydides dies and leaves his account of the Peloponnesian Wars behind.

Fourth Century BCE

399	The trial and subsequent execution of Socrates.
392	Aristophanes's *Assemblywomen* is produced.
388	Aristophanes's *Wealth* is produced.
384	Aristotle is born.
380	The death of Aristophanes. Plato establishes the Athens Academy.
370	The death of Hippocrates.
347	The death of Plato.
337	Macedonia's conquest of the Greek states is acknowledged at the League of Corinth.
336	Alexander takes over the reins of the empire. The age of Alexander the Great.
335	Aristotle founds the Lyceum in Athens.
330 (?)	Aristotle writes the *Poetics*.
322	The death of Aristotle.

BIBLIOGRAPHY/RECOMMENDED WORKS

Andrewes, A. *The Greek Tyrants*. London: Hutchinson University Library, 1956.

Aeschylus. *Aeschylus: The Complete Plays, Volume 1: Oresteia*. Translated by Carl R. Mueller. Hanover: Smith and Kraus Books, 2002.

Aeschylus. *Aeschylus, Plays One*. Translated by Frederic Raphael and Kenneth McLeish. London: Methuen Drama, 1991.

Aeschylus. *Eumenides*. Translated by E.D.A. Morshead. The Internet Classics Archive, 2009. http://classics.mit.edu/Aeschylus/eumendides.html (accessed May 13, 2009).

Aristotle. *Poetics*. Translated by Malcolm Heath. London: Penguin Books, 1996.

Aristotle. *The Politics and The Constitution of Athens*. Translated by Stephen Everson. Cambridge: Cambridge University Press, 1996.

Aristotle. *Aristotle's Rhetoric*. Translated by W. Rhys Roberts. The Internet Classics Archive, 2009. http://classics.mit.edu/Aristotle/rhetoric.html (accessed May 7, 2009).

Aristophanes. *Aristophanes, Plays One*. Translated by Patric Dickinson. Oxford: Oxford University Press, 1970.

Aristophanes. *Aristophanes: The Complete Plays*. Translated by Paul Roche. New York: New American Library, 2005.

Aristophanes. *Aristophanes, 1*. Edited by David R. Slavitt and Palmer Bovie. Philadelphia: University of Pennsylvania Press, 1998.

Bers, Victor, trans. *Demosthenes Speeches 50–59*. Austin: University of Texas Press, 2003.

Bowie, A.M. *Aristophanes: Myth, Ritual and Comedy*. Cambridge: Cambridge University Press, 1993.

Cahill, Thomas. *Sailing the Wine-Dark Sea: Why The Greeks Matter*. New York: Anchor Press, 2004.

Croiset, Maurice. *Aristophanes and the Political Parties At Athens*. Translated by James Loeb. London: Macmillan and Co., Limited, 1909.

Dearden, C.W. *The Stage of Aristophanes*. London: Athlone Press, 1976.

Downs, William M. and Lou Anne Wright. *Playwriting From Formula to Form: A Guide to Writing a Play*. Fort Worth, TX: Harcourt Brace College Publishers, 1998.

Euripides. *Grief Lessons: Four Plays by Euripides*. Translated by Anne Carson. New York: NYRB Classics, 2008.

Euripides. *Herakles Gone Mad: Rethinking Heroism in an Age of Endless War*. Translated by Robert Emmet Meagher. Northampton, MA: Olive Branch Press, 2006.

Euripides. *Hippolytus*. Translated by E.P. Coleridge. The Internet Classics Archive, 2009. http://classics.mit.edu/Euripides/hippolytus.html (accessed May 6, 2009).

Euripides, *Ten Plays by Euripides*. Translated by Moses Hadas and John McLean. New York: Bantam, 1990.

Finley, M.I. *Early Greece: The Bronze and Archaic Ages*. London: Chatto & Windus Ltd., 1981.

Garland, Robert. *Surviving Greek Tragedy*. London: Gerald Duckworth & Co., Ltd., 2004.

Goff, Barbara and Michael Simpson. *Crossroads in the Black Aegean*. Oxford: Oxford University Press, 2007.

Goldhill, Simon. *How To Stage Greek Tragedy Today*. Chicago: University of Chicago Press, 2007.

Grene, David and Richmond Lattimore, eds. *Euripides IV*. Chicago: University of Chicago Press, 1968.

Grene, David and Richmond Lattimore, eds. *Greek Tragedies, Volume 3*. Chicago: Phoenix Books, 1964.

Harriott, Rosemary M. *Aristophanes: Poet & Dramatist*. Baltimore: Johns Hopkins University Press, 1986.

Herington, John. *Aeschylus*. New York: Yale University Press, 1986.

Herodotus. *The Histories*. Translated by Robin Waterfield. Oxford: Oxford University Press, 1998.

Homer. *The Odyssey*. Translated by Robert Fagles. London: Penguin Books, 1996.

Laird, Andrew, ed. *Ancient Literary Criticism*. Oxford Readings in Classical Studies. Oxford: Oxford University Press, 2006.

Lloyd, Michael, ed. *Aeschylus*. Oxford Readings in Classical Studies. Oxford: Oxford University Press, 2006.

MacDowell, Douglas M. *Aristophanes and Athens: An Introduction to the Plays*. Oxford: Oxford University Press, 1995.

McHardy, Fiona, James Robson, and David Harvey, eds. *Lost Dramas of Classical Athens*. Exeter: University of Exeter Press, 2005.

Nicoll, Allardyce. *Masks, Mimes and Miracles: Studies in the Popular Theatre*. London: Harrap, 1931.

Parker, Geoffrey. *The World: An Illustrated History*. New York: Harper & Row, 1986.

Pausanias. *Descriptions of Greece*. Translated by J.G. Frazier. New York: Biblo and Tannen, 1965.

Plutarch. *Plutarch's Lives*. Translated by George Long and Aubrey Stewart. Project Gutenberg, 2009. http://www.gutenberg.org/files/14033/14033-h/14033-h.htm (accessed May 6, 2009).

Plutarch. *Plutarch's Lives*. Translated by George Long and Aubrey Stewart. Teddington, UK: Echo Library, 2007.

Rorty, Amélie Oksenberg, ed. *Essays on Aristotle's Poetics*. Princeton, NJ: Princeton University Press, 1992.

Rozik, Eli. *The Roots of Theatre: Rethinking Ritual and Other Theories of Origin*. Iowa City: University of Iowa Press, 2002.

Said, Suzanne and Monique Trédé. *A Short History of Greek Literature*. Translated by Trista Selous et al. New York: Routledge, 1999.

Sewell, Richard C. *In The Theatre of Dionysos: Democracy and Tragedy in Ancient Athens*. Jefferson, NC: McFarland & Company, Inc., 2007.

Sheffield Theatre Education Resource. http://www.sheffieldtheatres.co.uk/creativedevelopmentprogramme/productions/minotaur/theatre.shtml (accessed May 7, 2009).

Smith, Helaine L. *Masterpieces of Classic Greek Drama*. London: Greenwood Press, 2006.

Sophocles. *The Theban Plays: King Oedipus, Oedipus at Colonus, Antigone*. Translated by E.F. Watling. Baltimore: Penguin Classics, 1956.

Sophocles. *Sophocles, 1*. Edited by David R. Slavitt and Palmer Bovie. Philadelphia: University of Pennsylvania Press, 1998.

Sophocles. *Sophocles, 2*. Edited by David R. Slavitt and Palmer Bovie. Philadelphia: University of Pennsylvania Press, 1998.

Stinson, John. "Greek Theater, Plays Serve as Sources of Greek Culture." *Associated Content*, June 24, 2008. http://www.associatedcontent.com/article/806801/greek_theater_plays_serve_as_sources.html?cat=37 (accessed May 19, 2009).

Taplin, Oliver, ed. *Literature in the Greek and Roman Worlds: A New Perspective*. Oxford: Oxford University Press, 2000.

Thomson, George. *Aeschylus and Athens: A Study in the Social Origins of Drama*. New York: Haskell House Publishers, Ltd., 1967.

Thucydides. *The Complete Writings of Thucydides: The Peloponnesian War*. Translated by Richard Crawley. New York: Modern Library, 1951.

Thucydides. *The History of the Peloponnesian War.* Translated by Rex Warner. London: Penguin Books, 1972.

Walcot, Peter. *Greek Drama in its Theatrical and Social Context.* Cardiff: University of Wales Press, 1976.

Wise, Jennifer. *Dionysus Writes: The Invention of Theatre in Ancient Greece.* Ithaca, NY: Cornell University Press, 1998.

ACKNOWLEDGEMENTS

A number of individuals and organizations should be acknowledged.

I would like to thank Playwrights Canada Press first of all, and past publisher Angela Rebeiro for inciting this project. The present publisher, Annie Gibson, has been a great support and resource. In addition Leif Oleson Cormack, Meg Braem, Jim Dugan, the Banff Centre's Leighton Colony, and the Faculty of Fine Arts at the University of Calgary.

Clem Martini is an award-winning playwright, screen-writer, and novelist, a professor of drama at the University of Calgary, and a former president of the Playwrights Guild of Canada.